Small Business Tax Guide

Small Business Tax Guide

JOHN WHITELEY, F.C.A.

howtobooks

Acknowledgements
Crown Copyright material is reproduced with the permission of
the Controller of HMSO.

Published by How To Books Ltd,
3 Newtec Place, Magdalen Road,
Oxford OX4 1RE. United Kingdom.
Tel: (01865) 793806. Fax: (01865) 248780.
email: info@howtobooks.co.uk
www.howtobooks.co.uk

First published 2002
Updated and reprinted 2003

British Library Cataloguing in Publication Data
A catalogue record for this book is available from
the British Library

Produced for How To Books by Deer Park Productions
Edited by Diana Brueton
Typeset by PDQ Typesetting, Newcastle-under-Lyme, Staffs
Cover design by Baseline Arts Ltd, Oxford
Printed and bound by Cromwell Press, Trowbridge, Wiltshire

Contents

List of Illustrations

Preface

Running a small business has its problems, but also its rewards. It is satisfying to earn your living from your own efforts. But anybody running a small business wants to minimise the red tape, and maximise the results.

In this book I give you a guide to taxes generally, and to the main taxes affecting your business. I try to explain them in plain language, but more importantly I try to point out some of the opportunities to plan your business to make it more tax efficient. Never be tempted to put the cart before the horse, and run your business simply for the best tax breaks. But do not be blind to different ways of doing things which could save you tax.

I have drawn on over 25 years' experience in advising owners of small business to bring you this book. I do not promise to make you rich overnight, but this book will, I hope, help you plan your business in such a way that the taxman does not take an unduly large bite out of your money.

John Whiteley

1

Introduction

DEFINING YOUR GENERAL PHILOSOPHY

You are about to embark on a book about saving tax. Beware! This could prove to involve more of your life than just your financial arrangements. As with most things, a decision about one part of your life spills over to other parts. You could end up by re-evaluating your business – even your whole lifestyle.

You may have to pause over certain parts of the book, and ask 'Is this what I really want to do?' You may decide to throw yourself wholeheartedly into all the tax saving ideas. You may want to pick and choose the ones which relate to your circumstances. You may wish to bend your circumstances to be able to take advantage of some of the tax saving opportunities.

MAKING YOUR BUSINESS PLANS

You may take the attitude that tax is only a secondary matter. What matters most is what you want to do with your life. This is certainly a very wise opinion to hold. If you ran your whole life on the basis of what is the most tax efficient thing, it would truly be a case of the tail wagging the dog.

However, if you have embarked on a business or career, with a definite aim for your life, there may be occasions when you could do things in a more tax efficient manner, without getting the whole thing out of proportion. It makes no sense at all to neglect taking a few simple steps which could reduce your tax burden. In a judgement of a tax case which went to trial, a judge made the famous remark that nobody is under any obligation to order their affairs so that the Inland Revenue can put their biggest shovel into that person's wealth.

THE PERSONAL ANGLE

In thinking about tax planning – and, in fact, about any angle of your business – the thing that really matters is how it affects you and the other people involved in the business. As regards tax, what matters is how much you can get out of the company or business. The main taxes which impinge on that are **Income Tax**, **Capital Gains Tax** and **Inheritance Tax**. There is also **Corporation Tax**, which is a tax paid by companies – not people. This may have an effect on what you ultimately get out of the company, but only indirectly.

So in all your tax planning, think about the ultimate objective. This is the bottom line for you – after all the business activities, and all the various taxes, what is left for you?

DECIDING ON SCHEMES

From time to time you may see or hear of special schemes promoted as tax mitigation schemes. There are two types.

Officially sponsored schemes

Officially sponsored schemes, such as **ISAs** (individual savings accounts) or **Enterprise Incentive Schemes**, are government backed. They are schemes which have been devised by the government to encourage certain types of savings, or savings in general. By all means take advantage of these if you have enough money.

Privately sponsored schemes

The second type are privately sponsored schemes. They are
promoted by organisations which think they have found a
loophole that they can exploit. You may see them advertised
in the 'quality' press, or by private circulation of clients of tax
lawyers, accountants or investment houses. Be a little more
wary of these. They may well have a cost for joining the
scheme. The scheme may have been tried and tested, or it may
be untried. Get advice – and make sure it is independent
advice. Very often these schemes are targeted by the Inland
Revenue, and outlawed in the next Budget. Normally such
legislation is not retrospective, so if you have got in on a
scheme before it is outlawed your tax advantages are safe.

TAKING ADVICE FROM PROFESSIONALS

If you are in business, you probably have an accountant. Do
not look on him or her as just a glorified book keeper. A
qualified accountant can probably save you money in many
ways – and saving tax is just one of them.

Qualified or not?

Anybody can set up in business as an accountant, but only
people who are affiliated to the relevant institutes or
associations may call themselves Chartered Accountants or
Chartered Certified Accountants. Unqualified accountants
may be cheaper. However, qualified accountants have gone
through a rigorous process of training to become qualified,
and they must undergo a programme of continuing
professional education. They are also bound by strict ethical
codes, and are subject to disciplinary procedures if they fall
short, or if a complaint against them is upheld. In addition
they are required to take out professional indemnity
insurance to cover claims against them.

Specific advice

If you are a high net worth individual or business, you may also find it useful to take advice on an *ad hoc* basis for particular problems. For example, you may be contemplating selling an asset, and want to know the Capital Gains Tax implications. You may want to know how to pass on your wealth or business to the next generation of your family, and whether you can do it now, or if it has to wait until you die.

An accountant or tax lawyer could be of great use in these sort of circumstances. Very often the saving to you can far outweigh his or her fee.

Sometimes a specific action, such as making a trust which could be used as part of your tax saving plans, will need a solicitor to implement it, by drawing up the trust deed. It may also be that a life assurance policy might be taken out, as part of planning for inheritance tax. It would be useful to consult an independent financial adviser about life assurances.

GETTING YOUR PRIORITIES RIGHT

Do not let the tail wag the dog. The purpose of paying less tax is to have more left in your own pocket. In other words, it is the bottom line that counts. I make no apology for repeating this advice.

Therefore it is of no benefit to incur an expenditure purely for the purpose of getting tax relief. The maximum tax rate that you as an individual could suffer is 40% for Income Tax and Capital Gains Tax. What is the use of spending £100 simply to save £40 tax? You are still worse off to the tune of £60.

Having said this, there is sometimes a reason for bringing expenditure forward or putting it back, so that it is relieved in the tax year which is most beneficial to you (so long as it is expenditure you would have made anyway). But never be tempted to spend money you would not otherwise have done just so that you can get the tax relief.

2

Understanding the System

Whether or not you regard the taxman as the enemy, it is useful to know who you are dealing with, and how the system works.

THE INLAND REVENUE

The **Inland Revenue** administers:

- **Income Tax**
- **Corporation Tax**
- **Capital Gains Tax**
- **Inheritance Tax**
- and **Stamp Duty**.

It also has responsibility for collecting National Insurance contributions, and for administering statutory sick pay, statutory maternity pay and student loan repayments. VAT – **Value Added Tax** – is administered by the **Customs and Excise** and Council Tax and Business Rates are administered by the local authorities.

The Inland Revenue has local offices which deal with the administration of Corporation Tax, business accounts, **PAYE** (pay as you earn) and so on. Inland Revenue Inspectors deal with the work, with staff underneath them. There are various ranks of Inspectors and in each district there is a District Inspector in overall charge. The Inland Revenue also have various Accounts Offices, responsible for the collection of taxes.

There are also Commissioners of Income Tax. These are independent people appointed locally, who sit regularly to hear appeals and disputes between taxpayers and the Inland Revenue.

The Tax Year ends on 5 April each year for individuals and **partnerships**, and 31 March each year for **limited companies**.

CUSTOMS AND EXCISE

Customs and Excise is responsible for collecting customs duties and excise duties, as well as VAT. Because of their different constitution, they have different powers from the Inland Revenue and they go about their work in a different way.

Customs and Excise also has independent tribunals, based locally, to hear appeals and settle disputes between taxpayers and the Customs and Excise.

YOUR RESPONSIBILITIES

Although most individuals (about 18 million out of the 26 million taxpayers) pay their tax through the PAYE system, everybody has three main obligations:

1. To complete a self-assessment tax return when one is sent to you.

2. To notify the Inland Revenue if you have a source of income which is not already taxed, or a capital gain.

3. To keep adequate records relevant to enable you to make a correct and complete return of your income and capital gains.

Each of these obligations has time limits attached:

- The self-assessment tax return must be sent to the Inland Revenue by the later of either 31 January following the tax year to which it relates, or three months after it was sent to you.

- You must notify the Inland Revenue of a source of untaxed income or a capital gain by 5 October following the end of the tax year in which you received it.

- You must retain your records for 22 months from the end of the tax year to which they relate, unless you are in business or have property income, in which case you must retain them for five years and ten months from the end of the tax year to which they relate.

SELF-ASSESSMENT

Self-assessment has been around since the 1996/1997 tax year for individuals and partnerships, and since 2000 for companies. Here is a summary of the system.

INDIVIDUAL SELF-ASSESSMENT

A tax return may be sent to any individual. If you receive a tax return, you have an obligation to complete the return within the time limits stated above. The declaration which you must sign at the end of the tax return states that the tax return is correct and complete.

The main feature of the self-assessment system is that you, the taxpayer, are responsible for calculating your own tax, and paying it on the due dates. However, if you send it in before 30 September following the end of the tax year to which it relates (or within two months of receipt of the tax return if you received the tax return later than 30 September), you can request the Inland Revenue to work it out for you. Remember, though, that they are only calculating it as your agent. The final responsibility remains with you, the taxpayer.

The 30 September is also the deadline if you have to pay some tax and you would like it to be collected by the PAYE system in the following year.

The tax return form

The 'core' tax return form consists of eight pages, and there are supplementary pages for a further nine sections. The core pages are:

- Page 1 – This is the official notice from the Inland Revenue requiring you to make a return and giving you the dates by which you must submit it. It is sent from your local tax office, and gives details of where to get help.

- Page 2 (see Figure 1) – This is a questionnaire for you to work through. By ticking the appropriate boxes 'yes' or 'no', you will find out which supplementary page sections you need. The Inland Revenue should have sent you the supplementary pages which they think you might need by reference to the previous year's return. If you need any supplementary pages which were not sent with the tax return there is an orderline telephone number on this page to get them.

- Page 3 (see Figure 2) – This is to declare income from savings and investments. Enter here the income from the various types of investments – some of which have tax already deducted, and some of which do not. *Remember*, do not enter any income from tax exempt savings or investments such as **TESSAs**, **ISAs** or **PEPs**.

- Page 4 (see Figure 3) – This is to declare state pensions and benefits, other pensions and any other income not mentioned elsewhere. Again, some items will have tax deducted at source, while some items will be received gross.

- Page 5 (see Figure 4) – This is to claim reliefs. The top half of the page is to claim relief for the various types of pension contribution reliefs, and the bottom half to claim any other reliefs.

- Page 6 (see Figure 5) – This is to claim relief on gifts to charity (Question 15A).

- Pages 6 to 7 (see Figures 5 and 6) – This is to claim allowances – blind person's allowance, married couple's allowance, and the Child Tax Credit (Question 16). Question 17 is to declare any liability to make repayment of Student Loans or an Income Contingent Loan.

- Page 8 (see Figure 7) – This is to enter the calculation of tax payable (or repayable), and to give details of how you would like any overpayment of tax repaid to you.

- Page 9 (see Figure 8) – This is to declare other information such as your name and address, National Insurance number, and so on. Any additional information you wish to declare should be entered here in box 23.5 (which continues over the page).

- Page 10 (see Figure 9) – This is perhaps the most important part of the whole return. It is your declaration, which you should sign and date, that the return is correct and complete.

Supplementary pages

It is unlikely that you would need all nine supplementary page sections, but any of them could apply to you. You must decide which of the supplementary sections you need by looking at page 2 of the 'core' tax return (see Figure 1). The supplementary sections are:

- **Employment**. If you are employed, an office holder, a director, an agency worker, or received payments or

21

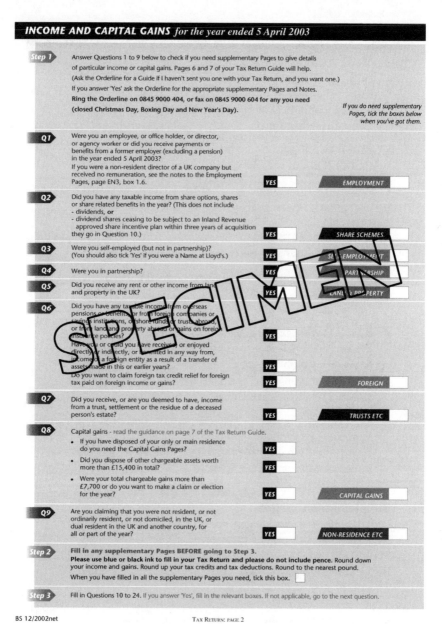

INCOME AND CAPITAL GAINS *for the year ended 5 April 2003*

Step 1 Answer Questions 1 to 9 below to check if you need supplementary Pages to give details of particular income or capital gains. Pages 6 and 7 of your Tax Return Guide will help.

(Ask the Orderline for a Guide if I haven't sent you one with your Tax Return, and you want one.)

If you answer 'Yes' ask the Orderline for the appropriate supplementary Pages and Notes.

Ring the Orderline on 0845 9000 404, or fax on 0845 9000 604 for any you need (closed Christmas Day, Boxing Day and New Year's Day).

If you do need supplementary Pages, tick the boxes below when you've got them.

Q1 Were you an employee, or office holder, or director, or agency worker or did you receive payments or benefits from a former employer (excluding a pension) in the year ended 5 April 2003?
If you were a non-resident director of a UK company but received no remuneration, see the notes to the Employment Pages, page EN3, box 1.6.
YES ☐   EMPLOYMENT ☐

Q2 Did you have any taxable income from share options, shares or share related benefits in the year? (This does not include
- dividends, **or**
- dividend shares ceasing to be subject to an Inland Revenue approved share incentive plan within three years of acquisition they go in Question 10.)
YES ☐   SHARE SCHEMES ☐

Q3 Were you self-employed (but not in partnership)?
(You should also tick 'Yes' if you were a Name at Lloyd's.)
YES ☐   SELF-EMPLOYMENT ☐

Q4 Were you in partnership?
YES ☐   PARTNERSHIP ☐

Q5 Did you receive any rent or other income from land and property in the UK?
YES ☐   LAND & PROPERTY ☐

Q6 Did you have any taxable income from overseas pensions or benefits, or from foreign companies or savings institutions, offshore funds or trusts abroad, or from land and property abroad or gains on foreign insurance policies?
YES ☐

Have you or could you have received or enjoyed directly or indirectly, or benefited in any way from, income of a foreign entity as a result of a transfer of assets made in this or earlier years?
YES ☐

Do you want to claim foreign tax credit relief for foreign tax paid on foreign income or gains?
YES ☐   FOREIGN ☐

Q7 Did you receive, or are you deemed to have, income from a trust, settlement or the residue of a deceased person's estate?
YES ☐   TRUSTS ETC ☐

Q8 Capital gains - read the guidance on page 7 of the Tax Return Guide.
- If you have disposed of your only or main residence do you need the Capital Gains Pages?
YES ☐
- Did you dispose of other chargeable assets worth more than £15,400 in total?
YES ☐
- Were your total chargeable gains more than £7,700 or do you want to make a claim or election for the year?
YES ☐   CAPITAL GAINS ☐

Q9 Are you claiming that you were not resident, or not ordinarily resident, or not domiciled, in the UK, or dual resident in the UK and another country, for all or part of the year?
YES ☐   NON-RESIDENCE ETC ☐

Step 2 **Fill in any supplementary Pages BEFORE going to Step 3.**
Please use blue or black ink to fill in your Tax Return and please do not include pence. Round down your income and gains. Round up your tax credits and tax deductions. Round to the nearest pound.
When you have filled in all the supplementary Pages you need, tick this box. ☐

Step 3 Fill in Questions 10 to 24. If you answer 'Yes', fill in the relevant boxes. If not applicable, go to the next question.

Fig. 1. Self-assessment tax return page 2.

INCOME *for the year ended 5 April 2003*

Q10 ▶ **Did you receive any income from UK savings and investments?**   **YES**

> If yes, tick this box and then fill in boxes 10.1 to 10.26 as appropriate. Include only your share from any joint savings and investments.
> If not applicable, go to Question 11.

■ *Interest*

● Interest from UK banks, building societies and deposit takers (interest from UK Internet accounts must be included) - *if you have more than one bank or building society etc. account enter totals in the boxes.*

- enter any bank, building society etc. interest that **has not** had tax taken off. (Most interest is taxed by your bank or building society etc. so make sure you should be filling in box 10.1, rather than boxes 10.2 to 10.4)

	Taxable amount
10.1	£

- enter details of your **taxed** bank or building society etc. interest. *The Working Sheet on page 10 of your Tax Return Guide will help you fill in boxes 10.2 to 10.4.*

Amount **after** tax deducted	Tax deducted	Gross amount **before** tax
10.2 £	**10.3** £	**10.4** £

● Interest distributions from UK authorised unit trusts and open-ended investment companies (dividend distributions go below)

Amount **after** tax deducted	Tax deducted	Gross amount before tax
10.5 £	**10.6** £	**10.7** £

● National Savings & Investments (other than First Option Bonds and Fixed Rate Savings Bonds and the first £70 of interest from an Ordinary Account)

	Taxable amount
10.8	£

● National Savings & Investments First Option Bonds and Fixed Rate Savings Bonds

Amount after tax deducted	Tax deducted	Gross amount before tax
10.9 £	**10.10** £	**10.11** £

● Other income from UK savings and investments (except dividends)

Amount after tax deducted	Tax deducted	Gross amount before tax
10.12 £	**10.13** £	**10.14** £

■ *Dividends*

● Dividends and other qualifying distributions from UK companies

Dividend/distribution	Tax credit	Dividend/distribution **plus** credit
10.15 £	**10.16** £	**10.17** £

● Dividend distributions from UK authorised unit trusts and open-ended investment companies

Dividend/distribution	Tax credit	Dividend/distribution **plus** credit
10.18 £	**10.19** £	**10.20** £

● Scrip dividends from UK companies

Dividend	Notional tax	Dividend **plus** notional tax
10.21 £	**10.22** £	**10.23** £

● Non-qualifying distributions and loans written off

Distribution/Loan	Notional tax	Taxable amount
10.24 £	**10.25** £	**10.26** £

Fig. 2. Self-assessment tax return page 3.

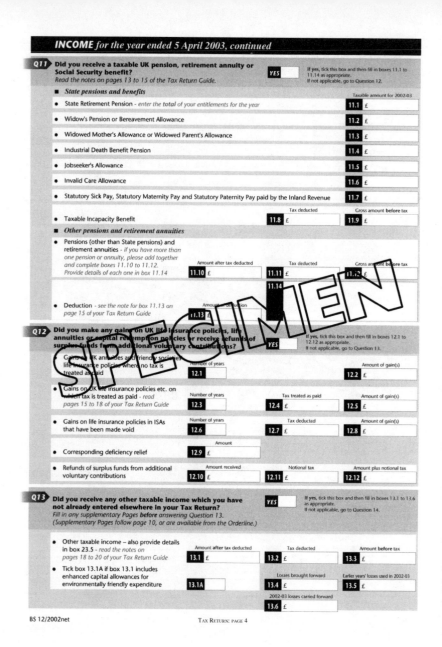

Fig. 3. Self-assessment tax return page 4.

Q14 **Do you want to claim relief for your pension contributions?** **YES** ☐   If yes, tick this box and then fill in boxes 14.1 to 14.11 as appropriate.
*Do **not** include contributions deducted from your pay by your employer to their pension scheme or associated AVC scheme, because tax relief is given automatically. But **do include** your contributions to personal pension schemes and Free-Standing AVC schemes.*   If not applicable, go to Question 15.

■ *Payments to your retirement annuity contracts - only fill in boxes 14.1 to 14.5 for policies taken out before 1 July 1988.*
See the notes on pages 20 and 21 of your Tax Return Guide.

Qualifying payments made in 2002-03	**14.1** £	2002-03 payments used in an earlier year	**14.2** £	Relief claimed box 14.1 *minus* (boxes 14.2 and 14.3, but not 14.4)
2002-03 payments now to be carried back	**14.3** £	Payments brought back from 2003-04	**14.4** £	**14.5** £

■ *Payments to your personal pension (including stakeholder pension) contracts - enter the amount of the payment you made with the basic rate tax added (the **gross** payment). See the note for box 14.6 on page 22 of your Tax Return Guide.*

Gross qualifying payments made in 2002-03   **14.6** £

2002-03 gross payments carried back to 2001-02   **14.7** £

Gross qualifying payments made between 6 April 2003 and 31 January 2004 brought back to 2002-03 - *see page 22 of your Tax Return Guide*   **14.8** £

Relief claimed box 14.6 *minus* box 14.7 (but not 14.8)   **14.9** £

■ *Contributions to other pension schemes and Free-Standing AVC schemes*

• Amount of contributions to employer's schemes **not deducted** at source from pay   **14.10** £

• Gross amount of Free-Standing Additional Voluntary Contributions paid in 2002-03   **14.11** £

Q15 **Do you want to claim any of the following reliefs?**
If you have made any annual payments, after basic rate tax, answer 'Yes' to Question 15 and fill in box 15.9. If you have made any gifts to charity go to Question 15A.   **YES** ☐   If yes, tick this box and then fill in boxes 15.1 to 15.12, as appropriate. If not applicable, go to Question 15A

• Interest eligible for relief on qualifying loans   **15.1** £

• Maintenance or alimony payments you have made under a court order, Child Support Agency assessment or legally binding order or agreement   **15.2** £   *Amount claimed up to £2,110*

To claim this relief, either you or your former spouse must have been 65 or over on 5 April 2000. So, if your date of birth, which is entered in box 22.6, is after 5 April 1935 then you must enter your former spouse's date of birth in box 15.2A - *see pages 23 and 24 of your Tax Return Guide*   **15.2A** / /   *Former spouse's date of birth*

• Subscriptions for Venture Capital Trust shares (up to £100,000)   **15.3** £   *Amount on which relief is claimed*

• Subscriptions under the Enterprise Investment Scheme (up to £150,000) - *also provide details in box 23.5, see page 24 of your Tax Return Guide*   **15.4** £   *Amount on which relief is claimed*

• Community Investment Tax relief - invested amount relating to previous tax year(s) and on which relief is due   **15.5** £

• Community Investment Tax relief - invested amount for current tax year   **15.6** £   *Total amount on which relief is claimed box 15.5 + box 15.6*   **15.7** £

• Post-cessation expenses, pre-incorporation losses brought forward and losses on relevant discounted securities, etc. - *see pages 24 and 25 of your Tax Return Guide*   **15.8** £   *Amount of payment*

• Annuities and annual payments   **15.9** £   *Payments made*

• Payments to a trade union or friendly society for death benefits   **15.10** £   *Half amount of payment*

• Payment to your employer's compulsory widow's, widower's or orphan's benefit scheme - *available in some circumstances – **first** read the notes on page 25 of your Tax Return Guide*   **15.11** £   *Relief claimed*

• Relief claimed on a qualifying distribution on the **redemption** of bonus shares or securities.   **15.12** £   *Relief claimed*

Fig. 4. Self-assessment tax return page 5.

ALLOWANCES *for the year ended 5 April 2003*

Q15A **Do you want to claim relief on gifts to charity?** **YES**
If you have made any Gift Aid payments answer 'Yes' to Question 15A. You should include Gift Aid payments to Community Amateur Sports Clubs here. You can elect to include in this Return Gift Aid payments made between 6 April 2003 and the date you send in this Return. See page 26 in the Tax Return Guide and the leaflet enclosed on Gift Aid.

If yes, tick this box and then read page 26 of your Tax Return Guide. Fill in boxes 15A.1 to 15A.5 as appropriate. If not applicable, go to Question 16.

- Gift Aid and payments under charitable covenants made between 6 April 2002 and 5 April 2003   **15A.1** £
- Enter in box 15A.2 the total of any 'one off' payments included in box 15A.1   **15A.2** £
- Enter in box 15A.3 the amount of Gift Aid payments made after 5 April 2003 but treated as if made in the tax year 2002-03   **15A.3** £
- Gifts of qualifying investments to charities – shares and securities   **15A.4** £
- Gifts of qualifying investments to charities – real property   **15A.5** £

Q16 **Do you want to claim blind person's allowance, married couple's allowance or the Children's Tax Credit?** **YES**
You get your personal allowance of £4,615 automatically. If you were born before 6 April 1938, enter your date of birth in box 22.6 - you may get a higher age-related personal allowance.

If yes, tick this box and then read pages 26 to 31 of your Tax Return Guide. Fill in boxes 16.1 to 16.33 as appropriate. If not applicable, go to Question 17.

	Date of registration (if first year of claim)		Local authority (or other register)
■ **Blind person's allowance**	**16.1** / /	**16.2**	

■ *Married couple's allowance - In 2002-03 married couple's allowance can only be claimed if either you, or your husband or wife, were born before 6 April 1935. So you can only claim the allowance in 2002-03 if either of you had reached 65 years of age before 6 April 2000. Further guidance is given beginning on page 27 of your Tax Return Guide.*

If **both** you and your husband or wife were born after 5 April 1935 you cannot claim; **do not** complete boxes 16.3 to 16.13.

If **you can claim** fill in boxes 16.3 and 16.4 if you are a married man or if you are a married woman and you are claiming half or all of the married couple's allowance.

- Enter your date of birth (if born before 6 April 1935)   **16.3** / /
- Enter your spouse's date of birth (if born before 6 April 1935 and older than you)   **16.4** / /

Then, if you are a married man fill in boxes 16.5 to 16.9. If you are a married woman fill in boxes 16.10 to 16.13.

- Wife's full name   **16.5**   • Date of marriage (if after 5 April 2002)   **16.6** / /

- Tick box 16.7, or box 16.8, if you or your wife have allocated half, or all, of the minimum amount of the allowance to her   Half **16.7**   All **16.8**

- Enter in box 16.9 the date of birth of any previous wife with whom you lived at any time during 2002-03. Read 'Special rules if you are a man who married in the year ended 5 April 2003' on page 28 before completing box 16.9.   **16.9** / /

- Tick box 16.10, or box 16.11, if you or your husband have allocated half, or all, of the minimum amount of the allowance to you   Half **16.10**   All **16.11**

- Husband's full name   **16.12**   • Date of marriage (if after 5 April 2002)   **16.13** / /

■ *Children's Tax Credit – even if you have already completed a separate Children's Tax Credit (CTC) claim form and received the relief in your tax code, you should still fill in boxes 16.14 to 16.26, as directed. Any reference to 'partner' in this question means the person you lived with during the year to 5 April 2003 – your husband or wife, or someone you lived with as husband or wife.*

Guidance for claiming CTC is on pages 28 to 31 of your Tax Return Guide. Please read the notes before completing your claim, particularly if either you, or your partner, were liable to tax above the basic rate in the year to 5 April 2003.

- Enter in box 16.14 the date of birth of a child living with you who was born on or after 6 April 1986. If you have a child living with you who was born on or after 6 April 2002 make sure you enter their date of birth in this box in preference to claiming for an older child.   **16.14** / /

- Tick box 16.15 if the child was your own child or one you looked after at your own expense. If not, you cannot claim CTC – go to box 16.27, if appropriate, or Question 17.   **16.15**

- Tick box 16.16 if the child lived with you **throughout** the year to 5 April 2003. If you ticked box 16.16 and
   - you were a lone or single claimant, you have finished this question; go to Question 17,
   - you have a partner, go to box 16.18.   **16.16**

- If the child lived with you for only **part of the year** you may only be entitled to a proportion of the CTC. Enter in box 16.17 your share in £s that **you have agreed** with any other claimants that may claim for this child. But leave boxes 16.17 to 16.25 blank if you separated from, or started living with, your partner during the year to 5 April 2003. Special rules apply to work out your entitlement; ask the Orderline for *Help Sheet IR343: Claiming Children's Tax Credit when your circumstances change* which explains how to complete box 16.26.   **16.17** £

BS 12/2002net   TAX RETURN: PAGE 6

Fig. 5. Self-assessment tax return page 6.

■ *Children's Tax Credit,* continued

If you lived with your partner (for CTC this means your husband or wife, or someone you lived with as husband and wife) for the whole of the year to 5 April 2003, fill in boxes 16.18 to 16.25 as appropriate.

- Enter in box 16.18 your partner's surname | **16.18**

- Enter in box 16.19 your partner's National Insurance number | **16.19**

- Tick
  - box 16.20 if **you** had the higher income in the year to 5 April 2003, | **16.20**
  or
  - box 16.21 if **your partner** had the higher income in that year | **16.21**

- Tick box 16.22 if either of you were chargeable to tax above the basic rate limit in the year to 5 April 2003. | **16.22**

*If you ticked boxes 16.20 and 16.22 your entitlement will be reduced – see page 30 of your Tax Return Guide; **your partner cannot claim CTC** - go to box 16.28, or Question 17 as appropriate.*

*If you ticked boxes 16.21 and 16.22 your partner s entitlement will be reduced; **you cannot claim CTC** – go to box 16.27, or Question 17, as appropriate.*

*If **neither** of you were chargeable above the basic rate and you had the lower income and*
- *you don't want to claim half of the entitlement to CTC, and*
- *you didn't make an election for CTC to go to the partner with the lower income*

you have finished this part of your Return - go to boxes 16.27 or 16.28, or Question 17, as appropriate (your partner should claim CTC if they have not already done so).

Otherwise, tick one of boxes 16.23 to 16.25 .

- I had the higher income and I am claiming all of our entitlement to CTC | **16.23**

- We are both making separate claims for half of our entitlement to CTC | **16.24**

- We elected before 6 April 2002, or because of our special circumstances during the year to 5 April 2003 (see page 31 of your Tax Return Guide), for the partner with the lower income to claim all of our entitlement to CTC | **16.25**

- If you separated from, or started living with, your partner in the year to 5 April 2003, enter in box 16.26 the amount of CTC you are claiming (following the guidance in Help Sheet IR343: Claiming Children's Tax Credit when your circumstances change). | **16.26** £

■ *Transfer of surplus allowances - see page 31 of your Tax Return Guide before you fill in boxes 16.27 to 16.33.*

- Tick box 16.27 if you want your spouse to have your unused allowances | **16.27**

- Tick box 16.28 if you want to have your spouse's unused allowances | **16.28**

- Tick box 16.29 if you want to have your partner's unused CTC | **16.29**

- Tick box 16.30 if your surplus CTC should be transferred to your partner | **16.30**

Please give details in the 'Additional information' box, box 23.5, on page 9 - *see page 31 of your Tax Return Guide for what is needed.*

If you want to calculate your tax, enter the amount of the surplus allowance you can have.

- Blind person's surplus allowance | **16.31** £

- Married couple's surplus allowance | **16.32** £

- Surplus CTC | **16.33** £

Q17 **Are you liable to make Student Loan Repayments for 2002-03 on an Income Contingent Student Loan?** *You must read the note on page 31 of your Tax Return Guide before ticking the 'Yes' box.* | **YES** | If yes, tick this box. If not applicable, go to Question 18.

If yes, and you are calculating your tax enter in Question 18, box 18.2A the amount you work out is repayable in 2002-03

Fig. 6. Self-assessment tax return page 7.

Q18 Do you want to calculate your tax and, if appropriate, any Student Loan Repayment?   **YES** ☐   Use your Tax Calculation Guide then fill in boxes 18.1 to 18.8 as appropriate.

- Unpaid tax for earlier years **included in your tax code for 2002-03**   **18.1** £ ☐

- Tax due for 2002-03 included in your tax code for a later year   **18.2** £ ☐

- Student Loan Repayment due   **18.2A** £ ☐

- Total tax, Class 4 NIC and Student Loan Repayment due for 2002-03 **before** you made any payments on account *(put the amount in brackets if an overpayment)*   **18.3** £ ☐

- Tax due for earlier years   **18.4** £ ☐

- Tax overpaid for earlier years   **18.5** £ ☐

- Tick box 18.6 if you are claiming to reduce your 2003-04 payments on account. Make sure you enter the **reduced** amount of your first payment in box 18.7. Then, in the 'Additional information' box, box 23.5 on page 9, say why you are making a claim   **18.6** ☐

- Your first payment on account for 2003-04 *(include the pence)*   **18.7** £ ☐

- Any 2003-04 tax you are reclaiming now   **18.8** £ ☐

Q19 Do you want to claim a repayment if you have paid too much tax? *(If you do not tick 'Yes' or the tax you have overpaid is below £10, I will use the amount you are owed to reduce your next tax bill.)*   **YES** ☐   If yes, tick this box and then fill in boxes 19.1 to 19.12 as appropriate. If not applicable, go to Question 20.

Should the repayment be sent:

- to your bank or building society account? *Tick box 19.1 and fill in boxes 19.3 to 19.7*   **19.1** ☐

or

- to your nominee's bank or building society account? *Tick box 19.2 and fill in boxes 19.3 to 19.12*   **19.2** ☐

We prefer to make repayment direct into a bank or building society account. (But tick box 19.8A or box 19.8B if you would like a cheque to be sent to you or your nominee.)

Name of bank or building society
19.3 ☐

Branch sort code
19.4 ☐

Account number
19.5 ☐

Name of account holder
19.6 ☐

Building society reference
19.7 ☐

If you would like a cheque to be sent to:

- you, at the address on page 1, tick box 19.8A   **19.8A** ☐

or

- your nominee, tick box 19.8B   **19.8B** ☐

If your nominee is your agent, tick box 19.9A   **19.9A** ☐

Agent's reference for you (if your nominee is your agent)
19.9 ☐

I authorise

Name of your nominee/agent
19.10 ☐

Nominee/agent address
19.11 ☐

            Postcode

to receive on my behalf the amount due

19.12 *This authority must be signed by you. A photocopy of your signature will not do.*

            Signature

Fig. 7. Self-assessment tax return page 8.

Acknowledgements
Crown Copyright material is reproduced with the permission of
the Controller of HMSO.

Published by How To Books Ltd,
3 Newtec Place, Magdalen Road,
Oxford OX4 1RE. United Kingdom.
Tel: (01865) 793806. Fax: (01865) 248780.
email: info@howtobooks.co.uk
www.howtobooks.co.uk

First published 2002
Updated and reprinted 2003

British Library Cataloguing in Publication Data
A catalogue record for this book is available from
the British Library

Produced for How To Books by Deer Park Productions
Edited by Diana Brueton
Typeset by PDQ Typesetting, Newcastle-under-Lyme, Staffs
Cover design by Baseline Arts Ltd, Oxford
Printed and bound by Cromwell Press, Trowbridge, Wiltshire

Small Business
Tax Guide

JOHN WHITELEY, F.C.A.

howtobooks

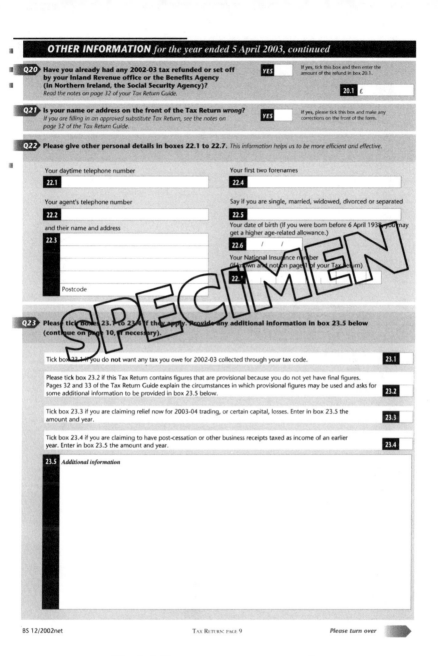

Q20 Have you already had any 2002-03 tax refunded or set off
by your Inland Revenue office or the Benefits Agency
(in Northern Ireland, the Social Security Agency)?
Read the notes on page 32 of your Tax Return Guide.

YES

If yes, tick this box and then enter the
amount of the refund in box 20.1.

20.1 £

Q21 Is your name or address on the front of the Tax Return *wrong*?
*If you are filling in an approved substitute Tax Return, see the notes on
page 32 of the Tax Return Guide.*

YES

If yes, please tick this box and make any
corrections on the front of the form.

Q22 Please give other personal details in boxes 22.1 to 22.7. *This information helps us to be more efficient and effective.*

Your daytime telephone number

22.1

Your agent's telephone number

22.2

and their name and address

22.3

Postcode

Your first two forenames

22.4

Say if you are single, married, widowed, divorced or separated

22.5

Your date of birth (If you were born before 6 April 1938, you may
get a higher age-related allowance.)

22.6   /   /

Your National Insurance number
(if known and not on page 1 of your Tax Return)

22.7

Q23 Please tick boxes 23.1 to 23.4 if they apply. Provide any additional information in box 23.5 below
(continue on page 10, if necessary).

Tick box 23.1 if you do **not** want any tax you owe for 2002-03 collected through your tax code.

23.1

Please tick box 23.2 if this Tax Return contains figures that are provisional because you do not yet have final figures.
Pages 32 and 33 of the Tax Return Guide explain the circumstances in which provisional figures may be used and asks for
some additional information to be provided in box 23.5 below.

23.2

Tick box 23.3 if you are claiming relief now for 2003-04 trading, or certain capital, losses. Enter in box 23.5 the
amount and year.

23.3

Tick box 23.4 if you are claiming to have post-cessation or other business receipts taxed as income of an earlier
year. Enter in box 23.5 the amount and year.

23.4

23.5 *Additional information*

Fig. 8. Self-assessment tax return page 9.

29

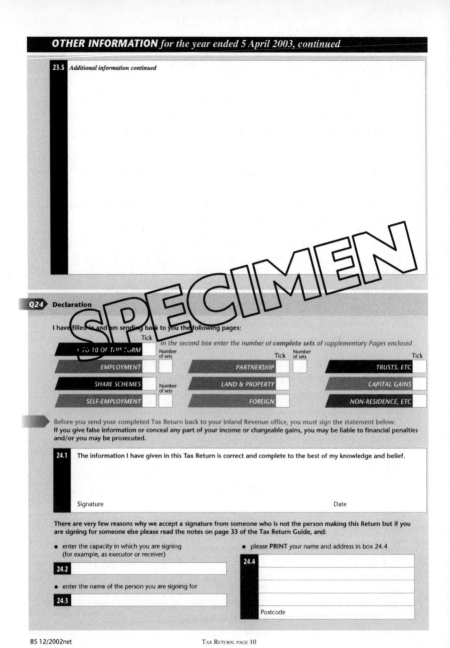

Fig. 9. Self-assessment tax return page 10.

benefits from a former employer (apart from a pension), you need these pages. On them you declare your salary, the tax deducted, other benefits and any expenses you claim.

- **Share schemes**. You need these pages if you have any taxable income from share option schemes, or share related benefits. Your employer would normally give you a statement of any such taxable figures.

- **Self-employment**. If you were self-employed on your own account, you need these pages. However, they do not include any income you have from a partnership. On these pages you declare your profits from your self-employment, and make your claims for capital allowances. If your business has a balance sheet you also enter the figures from the balance sheet here.

- **Partnership**. If you are a member of a partnership you must fill in these pages. There is a short version or a long version, depending on how many sources of income there are from the partnership. The partnership itself will have filled in a partnership self-assessment tax return, and this return will have allocated your share of the different types of income, or losses, to you. Make sure that the partner responsible for tax gives you the details of what your figures are. You must enter those figures on your own personal tax return.

- **Land and property**. These pages are used to declare income from land and property. This income may be Rent a Room, furnished holiday letting, or other income. Enter the income and the expenses and claims.

- **Foreign income**. Use these pages to declare any income from overseas. There are several pages in this section to declare income of different types.

- **Trusts**. These pages declare income from trusts, settlements, or a deceased person's estate.

- **Capital gains**. If you have disposed of any chargeable assets over a certain limit, you need these pages to give details. It may be that you have not made a profit from this, but a loss. You can still use these pages to claim the loss.

- **Non-residence**. If you claim non-residence, dual residence, or foreign domicile, you must use these pages to give details about yourself.

Paying the tax

Under the self-assessment system, you must not only assess your own tax, but you must also pay the tax on time. Although the onus is again on you, the Inland Revenue do provide you with a reminder. They issue a statement of account (rather like a credit card statement) whenever some tax is coming up for payment. This statement will show the amount to pay and the due date for payment (see Figure 10). The bottom part of the statement is in the form of a payslip, which you can use to make the payment. Payment may be made by several methods:

- **By post**. You may send your cheque with the payslip to the Inland Revenue Accounts Office – a prepaid envelope is sent with all statements of account.

- **By Bank Giro Credit**. The payslip is in a form to enable you to do this.

- **By debit card**. Telephone 0845 305 1000. (See Figure 11.)

- **Electronically**. After initial problems it is now possible to pay your tax electronically, but only if you have filed your tax return over the Internet. There is a one-off discount of £10 if you do this. Full details are on the Inland Revenue's website – www.inlandrevenue.gov.uk.

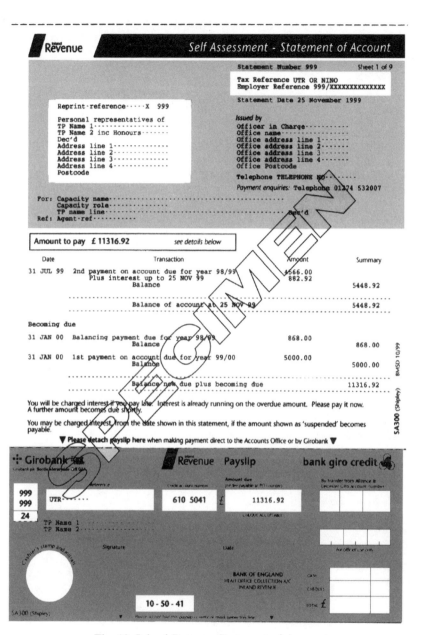

Fig. 10. Inland Revenue Statement of Account.

 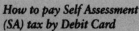

*How to pay Self Assessment
(SA) tax by Debit Card*

If you have a Switch **S** Solo **S** or Visa Delta debit card

you can pay your SA tax by telephoning **0845 305 1000**.
Phone us any day between 8.00 a.m. and 10.00 p.m. *See note 3 below*

Advantages of paying by debit card

- It is convenient – you only have to pick up the phone
- Saves writing cheques and visiting the bank or post office.
- Provides greater certainty that your payment has reached us.

Before you phone you will need

- Your debit card.
- Your 10 digit SA reference number (shown on the payslip attached to your statement).
- Details of the amount you are to pay.

☎ *When* you phone 0845 305 1000 the operator will

- Ask for details of your Debit Card, SA reference number and the amount you are paying.
- Take a note of your name, and may ask for your address and telephone number.
- Give you an authorisation code to confirm your payment has been processed.

Your call may be recorded to maintain and improve the quality of our service.

Notes
1 All calls to the debit card number are charged at the local rate.
2 If you are unsure how much to pay, telephone your local tax office. The telephone number is shown on the top
   right hand portion of your taxpayer statement.
3 The debit card payment telephone line is not open on 25 December 1999, 31 December 1999 and
   1 January 2000.
4 If you telephone and hear the engaged tone, please try again later. Our lines are busy at peak times.

SA342   41062 10.99 Niceday Stationery & Print Limited   86/SD10/99   R002000

Fig. 11. Form SA 342.

Here are some do's and dont's of paying your tax –

Do
- Send your payment to the accounts office – not to your local tax office.

- Send a letter to your local tax office if you want your payment split between different tax years.

- Attach a note of explanation if the cheque is post-dated.

- Send separate personalised payslips if the cheque covers more than one taxpayer.

- Make sure that the total amount is correct if the cheque covers more than one taxpayer.

- Use the pre-printed payslip and envelope whenever possible.

- If a payslip is not available write your tax reference, and your name and address on the back of the cheque.

- Use separate payslips for each partner in a partnership.

Don't
- Use somebody else's payslip.

- Use a photocopy of a payslip.

- Write to the accounts office querying amounts shown on the payslip, or explaining why the payment differs from the pre-printed amount on the payslip.

- Use a partnership tax reference for payment if no payslip is available.

The tax payments are made on a basis of payments on account and a final balancing payment (or refund).

Payments on account

The payments on account are paid on 31 January falling in the tax year, and 31 July after the tax year, and are based on the amount of income tax (but not capital gains tax), and Class 4 National Insurance you paid in the previous year (apart from any tax deducted at source).

Example

Your tax liability for 2002/2003 was £2,000, of which £200 was tax deducted at source. Your payments on account for 2003/2004 are based on the balance of £1,800, and you will have to pay £900 on 31 January 2004, and £900 on 31 July 2004.

You do not have to make payments on account if:

- 80 per cent or more of your total tax for the previous year was deducted at source, or
- the total payments on account would be less than £500.

Balancing payments

When you have made your self-assessment and sent the tax return to the Inspector of Taxes, you have arrived at a calculation of the tax for the year. If that tax figure is more than the amounts already paid on account, a balancing payment is due on 31 January following the end of the tax year. This is on the same date as the first payment on account for the following year, and the two amounts are paid together.

Example

Your final tax liability for 2002/2003 year comes to £2,200, of which £200 was tax deducted at source, leaving a liability to pay of £2,000. You have already made payments on account totalling £1,800. The tax payments you must make are as follows:

31 January 2004	Balancing payment for 2002/2003	£200
	1st payment on account for 2003/2004	£1,000
	Total due	£1,200
31 July 2004	2nd payment on account for 2003/2004	£1,000

Balancing refunds

If the final tax liability is less than the payments on account, a balancing refund is due. This is usually done at the same time as the first payment on account for the following year.

Example
Your final tax liability for 2002/2003 year comes to £1,600, of which £200 was tax deducted at source, leaving a liability to pay of £1,400. You have already made payments on account totalling £1,800. The tax payments you must make are as follows:

31 January 2004	Balancing refund for 2002/2003	£400
	1st payment on account for 2003/2004	£700
	Net amount due	£300
31 July 2004	2nd payment on account for 2003/2004	£700

Reducing the payments on account

If you have good reason to believe that the tax liability for the following year will be less than the previous year, or even nil, you can claim to reduce the payments on account. You must use the Inland Revenue form SA303 to do this (see Figure 12). Do not do this if the new figure you suggest is unrealistic. If you do not pay enough on the payments on account, there will be an interest charge on the amounts you should have paid.

Example
Your tax liability for 2002/2003 was £2,000, of which £200 was tax deducted at source. Your payments on account for 2003/2004 would be based on the balance of £1,800, and you would have to pay £900 on 31 January 2004, and £900

If this box is blank please enter your Tax reference, Employer reference or National Insurance number, from the top right hand corner of your Statement of Account.	Tax reference Employer reference National Insurance number

Inland Revenue office name and address
from the top of your Statement of Account

Please read the notes overleaf before completing this form

Tax year to which
this claim relates | — |

Example, enter the tax year ending 5 April 2002 as | *2001 — 02* |

Taxpayer's name & address *unless shown above*
Use CAPITAL LETTERS

Full name

Address

Postcode

SPECIMEN

I believe that

The total Income Tax and Class 4 National Insurance
contributions (NICs)* payable for the tax year of
claim (minus any tax deducted at source) **will be
less than** the payments on account based on the
previous tax year

or

There will be no Income Tax or Class 4 NICs* due
for the tax year of claim

* *Ignore Capital Gains Tax and Student Loan repayments*

My reason(s)

The business profits are down ... ...
Other income has gone down ... ...
The tax allowances and reliefs have gone up
The tax deducted at source is more than in the
previous tax year

Other reason *please specify*

**I wish to reduce each
payment on account for
the tax year of claim to** £

*Each reduced payment on account should be half
of the net Income Tax and Class 4 NICs you expect
to have to pay for the tax year.*

I understand that

- if the payments on account finally due
  are greater than the amounts paid,
  interest will be charged on the difference

- **any false information given may result in
  financial penalties.**

Signature

Date | / | / |

If form signed by agent please enter the following:

Agent's
name

Agent's
reference

Agent's
telephone
number

*When you have completed and signed this form
send it to your Inland Revenue office.*

SA303

BS 10/01

Fig. 12. Form SA 303.

on 31 July 2004. However, you claim to reduce the payments on account to £500 each. Your final self-assessment for 2003/2004 shows a liability of £2,200, of which tax deducted at source is £200. Your payments are therefore:

31 January 2004	1st payment on account for 2003/2004	£500
31 July 2004	2nd payment on account for 2003/2004	£500
31 January 2005	Balancing payment for 2003/2004	£1,000
31 January 2005	1st payment on account for 2004/2005	£1,000
31 July 2005	2nd payment on account for 2004/2005	£1,000

Thus the total payment due on 31 January 2005 will be £2,000. However, because you claimed to reduce the payments on account, but the final tax liability proved not to be as low as you expected, there will be interest to pay. This is calculated on the difference between the amount you should have paid based on the previous year's liability, and the amount you actually paid. This difference is £400 for each payment on account, so interest is calculated at the official rate on £400 from 31 January 2004, and on £400 from 31 July 2004.

Correcting mistakes

If you discover any mistakes on your tax return, you may correct them up to one year from the latest filing date applicable to your return. You do this by simply writing to the Inspector of Taxes and informing them of the error. However, if your tax return has been chosen for an enquiry, you are precluded from doing this.

The Inspector of Taxes may also correct any obvious mistakes which they find. This includes things like a wrong figure carried from one box or another, and arithmetical errors. They must do this within nine months of receiving your tax return, and must inform you of the corrections made. They will also tell you of the corrected amount of tax due to be paid.

Enquiries

As part of the control system of self-assessment, the Inspector of Taxes has the right to make enquiries into your tax return. They must do this within certain time limits:

- If you have filed your tax return on time they have one year from the last filing date (normally 31 January following the tax year).

- If you have filed your tax return late they have a year from the next quarter date after you filed your return. The quarter dates are 31 January, 30 April, 31 July and 31 October.

These enquiries may be on a random basis, or they may be prompted by some feature or aspect of the figures. The latter enquiries are known as 'aspect enquiries'. If an aspect enquiry is satisfactorily answered, that enquiry will normally be closed down and the tax return agreed. You have no right to challenge the right of the Inspector of Taxes to make an enquiry, so long as they have started it and informed you within the time limit.

A random enquiry will usually seek to verify all of the entries on the tax return. Under this type of enquiry the Inspector of Taxes has the right to call for any information or records. However, they must specify a time limit for you to produce any documents, which must not be less than 30 days. The Inspector of Taxes may also require you to attend an interview. This would normally be at their office, but you may request that the interview be at your home or place of business. The Inspector of Taxes will usually agree to this if you are unable to travel through incapacity or some other good cause.

It is usually in your best interest to get the enquiry cleared up as quickly as possible, and the Inspector of Taxes will also want to do this. Always remember these golden rules for dealing with an enquiry:

- If you are aware of any mistake or anything you have not declared, make a full disclosure straight away. If there is a later settlement the penalties will be less if you have co-operated as early as possible.

- At an interview just answer the questions – do not volunteer any further information.

- Always remain courteous.

- Be prepared to discuss a settlement figure if there has been any income not declared.

- Remember that the Inspector of Taxes can extend the enquiry into earlier years if they have reason to believe that any mistakes or under-declarations were not isolated.

When you and the Inspector of Taxes have agreed that all the enquiries are completed, they will issue you with a notice confirming that the enquiry is ended. They will also tell you if there are any adjustments to make to your self-assessment, if there are any under-declarations of tax – or indeed any over-declarations. You then have 30 days to amend your self-assessment. But you also have the opportunity to revise any claims you have previously made (such as capital allowance claims, etc) whether on the original return or in the course of the enquiry.

If you believe that the enquiry should be closed down, but the Inspector of Taxes do not agree, you have the right to ask the Commissioners to issue a notice ordering the Inspector of Taxes to close the enquiry. If the Commissioners agree with you they will issue such a notice, but of course the Inspector of Taxes have the right to tell the Commissioners why they think that the enquiry should not yet be closed down.

Agreeing a settlement

If the Inspector of Taxes have discovered that additional tax is due, and that you did not disclose all the facts, they may seek a 'contract settlement'. This may include interest and penalties. There are fixed penalties for such things as failing to comply with notices to supply information or documents, but there are also penalties geared to the amount of tax under-declared.

The tax-geared penalties start at 100% of the tax under-declared, but they are reduced for different elements, including:

- Disclosure, ie whether you have voluntarily disclosed information to the Inspector of Taxes.

- Degree of co-operation.

- Size and gravity of the case.

In theory, if all these elements were fully in your favour the penalty would be reduced to nil. If you think that the penalty is too harsh, taking into account your conduct of the enquiry, you may challenge the calculation of the penalty and negotiate it down.

When the settlement has been finally agreed you will be asked to sign a statement of full disclosure and a statement of assets. The statement of full disclosure certifies that you have disclosed to the Inspector of Taxes all the facts that are relevant to the calculation of your tax for the period covered by the enquiry. The statement of assets shows all your private and business assets.

SELF-ASSESSMENT FOR PARTNERSHIPS

Each partnership will receive a partnership self-assessment tax return separately from the individual members of the partnership. That tax return shows similar details to the self-employment supplementary pages of an individual's tax return. It shows details of the profit, claims for capital allowances, etc. However, it also has a section to show the tax details of each partner, and their share of the profits (or losses) and of any other income of the partnership. The partnership tax return should also give details of any chargeable assets disposed of, and the way in which the proceeds are shared amongst the partners. Each individual partner is then responsible for calculating their share of any capital gain or loss on that disposal.

A partnership must nominate one partner who is responsible for taxation matters. That partner is responsible for the partnership self-assessment tax return, and should inform the other partners of the entries made on the partnership tax return so that they can make the proper entries on their individual tax returns.

SELF-ASSESSMENT FOR CORPORATION TAX

Self-assessment for companies has been in force for all accounting periods ending after 1 July 1999. The principle is similar to that for individuals.

Corporation Tax return

The Corporation Tax return (CT600) has to be completed and submitted to the Inland Revenue by the later of either:

- 12 months after the end of the accounting period, or
- three months after the notice of return has been issued.

The return form consists of 12 pages, and there are seven sets of supplementary pages. The 'core' return consists of eight sections:

1. Notes to help you decide which supplementary pages you need.
2. Declaration of turnover.
3. Short calculation.
4. Detailed calculation.
5. Claims for Capital Allowances and Research and Development.
6. Losses, deficits and excesses.
7. Repayment claims.
8. Details of directors' remuneration.

The first page is for general information about the company, and the declaration which must be signed by a director or any other person authorised to sign by the company. The return must be accompanied by:

- the company's financial statements (accounts)
- the directors' report
- the auditor's report (if applicable)
- calculations showing how figures on the return have been arrived at, where these are different from the figures in the financial statements.

Enquiries

The Inland Revenue have the same right to make enquiries into Corporation Tax returns as they have for individuals. They have 12 months from the date of filing of a return. Once this period has passed they can only open an enquiry if they have made a discovery. The Inland Revenue have indicated that they are likely to make more enquiries into companies under self-assessment than previously. However, they have also indicated that they will target companies which they believe show a greater risk of loss of tax to the Revenue. This could include such factors as:

- cash-based businesses
- frequent transactions with overseas companies
- owner-managed companies, and
- companies with a bad record of compliance (eg with PAYE regulations).

Payment of Tax

The payment of Corporation Tax is determined by the size of the company's profit. If the profit is above the limit for the 30% rate of tax (currently £1,500,000), the tax is payable in four instalments. The limit of £1,500,000 is reduced proportionately where two or more companies are 'associated'. Associated means that one company controls others, or they are all controlled by the same person or group of people.

Example
If there are five associated companies, the limit for each of them for these purposes is £300,000.

The four instalments should be made as follows:

- The first instalment is made six months and 13 days after the start of the accounting period.

- The second and third instalments are then made at three-monthly intervals after the first instalment.

- The fourth instalment is made three months and 14 days after the end of the accounting period.

The instalments are made on the basis of the estimated liability to Corporation Tax. If there is any balance remaining after the four instalments have been made, it should be paid by nine months and one day after the end of the accounting period. Any overpayment on the instalments will be repaid.

Other companies
For all companies whose profits do not exceed the limit for
the 30% Corporation Tax rate, the tax is payable nine
months and one day after the end of the accounting period.

Interest

Interest is payable on any underpaid tax or instalment at the
current base rate plus 1%. If tax is overpaid, credit interest
is given at the base rate less ¼%. If interest is paid on
underpaid tax, it is allowable as an expense against taxable
profits.

TAX EFFICIENCY AUDIT

1. Do you have a system to record all the information you
   need for your tax return?

2. Do you keep all the documents needed?

3. How can you be sure you have enough money to pay the
   tax bill when it becomes due?

3

General Principles of Tax Planning

The general principles of tax planning involve making sure
you use all your personal allowances, credits, reliefs and the
lowest possible rates of tax. They apply to all individuals,
whether in business or not, and this chapter gives details of
all the allowances, credits and reliefs. Not all of them may
be applicable to you, but they give an overall view of what is
available.

USING YOUR ALLOWANCES

Personal tax allowances are claimed by completing the right
part of the self-assessment tax return. Therefore the first
and most obvious way to pay less tax is to make sure that
you claim all the allowances to which you are entitled. The
allowances available are:

- **Personal** allowance.
- **Higher age related personal** allowance.
- **Higher age related married couple's** allowance.
- **Blind person's** allowance.

How do you claim allowances?
Allowances are claimed by completing the appropriate box
on pages 6 and 7 of your self-assessment tax return (see
Figures 5 and 6).

Personal allowance

Personal allowance is given to everybody. You do not have to reach any particular age to qualify for it. It is given to you from the moment you are born. For the 2003/2004 tax year the personal allowance is £4,615. As we shall see, it is a key element in planning to pay less tax.

Tax Tip
Make sure that, as far as possible, you and everybody in your family uses up their personal tax allowance.

The personal allowance is usually increased each year by at least the same percentage as inflation. All other allowances have to be claimed on the tax return.

Higher age related personal allowance

If you are over 65 at the end of the tax year, you can claim the higher age related personal allowance. In order to do this you must enter your date of birth on the tax return. There are two rates of higher allowance:

- £6,610 for 2003/2004 if you are aged between 65 and 74 at the end of the tax year, and
- £6,720 for 2003/2004 if you are aged 75 or over at the end of the tax year.

How do you claim higher age allowance?
To claim the higher age allowance enter your date of birth in box 22.6 on page 9 of your self-assessment tax return (see Figure 8).

Restriction on higher age related allowances

If your annual income is over a certain level, the higher age related allowance is restricted. For the 2003/2004 tax year the income level is £18,300 per year. The restriction operates by reducing your allowance by one half of the excess of your income over the limit.

48

Example
You are aged 65 in the tax year. Your total income for the year is £18,700. The calculation is as follows:

Normal allowance		6,610
Income	18,700	
Restriction level	18,300	
Excess over level	400	
One half excess		200
Restricted allowance		£6,410

The allowance cannot however be restricted to an amount less than the normal personal allowance for a person under 65. If the restriction would bring the allowance down to a figure less than this, the allowance is restricted only as far as the normal personal allowance.

Example
You are aged 77 in the tax year. Your income is £25,700. The calculation is as follows:

Normal age allowance		6,720
Income	25,700	
Restriction level	18,300	
Excess	7,400	
One half excess		3,700
Restricted allowance		£3,020

But the allowance cannot be restricted below the lower personal allowance of £4,615.

How do you restrict your higher age allowance?
This is part of the process of calculation of tax. It is not done by ticking a box. If you calculate the tax the calculation guide takes you through the steps. If you get your tax return in early enough the Inspector of Taxes calculates your tax.

Marginal rate of tax

It is not hard to see that if you are entitled to a higher age related allowance, then once your income is above the restriction level you are paying a higher marginal rate of tax.

Example

You are aged 65 and your total income for the year is £19,300. Compare the tax payable with that payable if your income was £18,300.

Income			19,300
Normal age allowance		6,610	
Income	19,300		
Restriction level	18,300		
Excess	1,000		
One half excess		500	
Restricted allowance			6,110
Taxable			£13,190
Tax – 10% on £1,960		196.00	
– 22% on £11,230		2,470.60	
Total		£2,666.60	

Comparison:		
Income		18,300
Age allowance		6,610
Taxable		£11,690
Tax – 10% on £1,960	196.00	
– 22% on £9,730	2,140.60	
Total	£2,336.60	

Thus the total tax on income of £19,300 is £2,666.60, and on income of £18,300 it is £2,336.60. There is extra tax of £330 to pay on extra income of £1,000. This means that the top £1,000 of income has suffered tax at 33%.

Tax tip
Keep income out of this band that is taxed at a higher rate.
Here is one way to do this.

How can you keep income out of the higher marginal rate?
Income from an insurance 'bond', if restricted to 5%
withdrawals of the amount invested, is not taken into
account for tax purposes. The withdrawals up to 5% are
effectively accumulated for up to 20 years. Thus if you had
income in, say, a building society account earning interest at
5%, and this took you over the limit for restriction of the
higher age allowance, you could take the money out and put
it in an insurance bond, and still draw the same 5% income.
For tax purposes, however, that income would not be taxed
and you would have saved tax at 33% on the income you
draw.

Question
Is it worthwhile reducing my income to keep out of this
marginal tax rate?

Answer
Never deliberately reduce your income or incur an expense
just to save tax. You are still losing out. For example, if you
reduced your income to avoid the marginal rate of 33%
mentioned above, you would still be worse off to the extent
of 67 pence for every pound by which you reduced your
income.

Above the marginal rate
Once your income is above the marginal rate, (ie it is above
the maximum restriction limit), any further increase in your
income would have no effect on the rate of tax you suffer
until you hit the threshold for the higher rate of tax – 40%.

Summary of tax bands

If you are over 65 the tax rates on your income, after deduction of your personal allowance, fall into several distinct bands, depending on the type of income:

Tax Rates

Income	Earned		Interest		Dividends	
Age	65+	75+	65+	75+	65+	75+
up to £1,960	10%	10%	10%	10%	10%	10%
from £1,961 to £18,300	22%	22%	20%	20%	10%	10%
from £18,301 to £22,290	33%		30%		15%	
from £18,301 to £22,510		33%		30%		15%
from £22,291 to £30,500	22%		20%		10%	
from £22,511 to £30,500		22%		20%		10%
above £30,500	40%	40%	40%	40%	32.5%	32.5%

Age related married couple's allowance

The married couple's allowance for people under 65 was abolished from 6 April 2000, but if either spouse is over 65 the married couple's allowance depends on the age of the older spouse at the end of the tax year. The allowances for 2003/2004 are:

- £5,565 if the older spouse is between 65 and 74 at the end of the tax year

- £5,635 if the older spouse is 75 or over at the end of the tax year.

The relief is given at 10%.

How do you claim married couple's allowance?
Enter your date of birth in box 16.3 on page 6 (see Figure 5) and your wife's date of birth in box 16.4 on page 6 (see Figure 5) of your self-assessment tax return.

Restriction on higher married couple's allowance

The higher age allowance for married couples is also restricted if the income is over the restriction level (£18,300 for 2003/2004). The restriction is one half of the excess over £18,300, less any restriction already applied to the personal allowance.

The same band of income taxed at a higher marginal rate can therefore also occur due to this restriction.

USING YOUR TAX CREDITS

From 6 April 2001 various tax credits were introduced.

Children's Tax Credit and Working Tax Credit

Confusingly, although these are described as tax credits, they are actually a benefit given to the main person responsible for a child or children in a family (in the case of Child Tax Credit), or to people who are employed or self-employed (in the case of Working Tax Credit). The credits are means tested, but given where the joint household income is £58,000 or less (£66,000 or less if a child is less than one year old).

Child Tax Credit
This is a benefit for people responsible for at least one child or qualifying young person. For couples, the credit is paid to the person mainly responsible for caring for the child. For a lone parent, it is paid directly to that person.

Working Tax Credit
This is a benefit for people either self-employed or employed, who:

- usually work at least 16 hours per week,
- are paid for that work, and

- expect to work for at least four weeks, and are
  - aged 16 or over and responsible for at least one child, or
  - aged 16 or over and disabled, or
  - aged 25 or over and usually work at least 30 hours per week.

A claim must be made for these credits on form TC600 – available from local tax offices, or on the Internet at www.taxcredits.inlandrevenue.gov.uk/Home.aspx. The website also allows you to enter your details to see if you qualify.

This system involves the claimant in obligations:

- to inform the Inland Revenue of various changes in circumstances,
- to file end of year compliance forms, and
- to face the possibility of a Tax Credit enquiry.

Tax tip
Initially, claims are made on the basis of the income of the previous year. It could be possible therefore that the income of the previous year would restrict the benefit, but for the current year would be less, and the benefit would be greater. However, to claim the benefit, a claim must be made by 5 July in the tax year for the benefit to be paid for the whole of that tax year. Thereafter, claims can only be backdated three months.

It is a good idea therefore to make a claim even if the income of the previous year was too high. An initial award of nil will be made, but if the income then proves to be lower, it can be adjusted. This adjustment will then apply for the whole of the tax year. By contrast, if the claim is only made when the circumstances are known, the award can only be backdated three months, and potentially much of the benefit would be lost.

CAPITAL ALLOWANCES

If you use an asset for your business or your work, you may claim **capital allowances** as a deduction from your income for tax purposes.

If you use the asset partly for business and partly for private use the allowance is worked out in the normal way, but only the business proportion is given as a deduction from your income.

How do you claim capital allowances?
Claim capital allowances by entering the amount in box 1.35 of page 2 of the employment pages (see Figure 13), or boxes 3.14 to 3.23 on page 1 of the self-employment pages (see Figure 14).

What items can you claim capital allowances on?

There is really no restriction on what assets you can claim on. It could be something as small as a hand drill, or as large as an aeroplane. The only test is that it is used for business purposes. If there is any private usage the proportion of allowances claimable is limited to the business proportion only.

Capital allowances are broadly similar to providing for depreciation on these assets used for your business. However, at certain times the government announces higher rates of capital allowances than the normal 25%. For instance, from July 1997 to June 1998 the rate of allowance for the first year of claiming for an asset was 50%, and since July 1998 it has been 40%. There is also a 100% allowance for expenditure on

- computers and similar equipment
- plant and machinery meeting strict water saving or energy efficiency criteria.

55

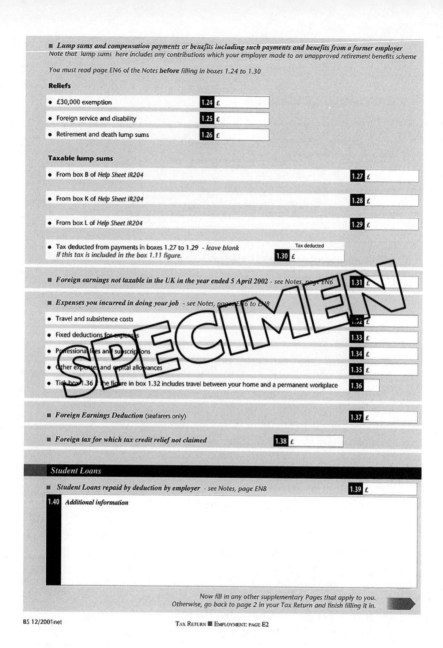

■ *Lump sums and compensation payments or benefits including such payments and benefits from a former employer*
Note that lump sums here includes any contributions which your employer made to an unapproved retirement benefits scheme

*You must read page EN6 of the Notes **before** filling in boxes 1.24 to 1.30*

Reliefs

• £30,000 exemption	**1.24**	£
• Foreign service and disability	**1.25**	£
• Retirement and death lump sums	**1.26**	£

Taxable lump sums

• From box B of *Help Sheet IR204*	**1.27**	£
• From box K of *Help Sheet IR204*	**1.28**	£
• From box L of *Help Sheet IR204*	**1.29**	£
• Tax deducted from payments in boxes 1.27 to 1.29 - leave blank if this tax is included in the box 1.11 figure.	Tax deducted **1.30** £	

■ *Foreign earnings not taxable in the UK in the year ended 5 April 2002* - see Notes, page EN6 **1.31** £

■ *Expenses you incurred in doing your job* - see Notes, pages EN6 to EN8

• Travel and subsistence costs	**1.32**	£
• Fixed deductions for expenses	**1.33**	£
• Professional fees and subscriptions	**1.34**	£
• Other expenses and capital allowances	**1.35**	£
• Tick box 1.36 if the figure in box 1.32 includes travel between your home and a permanent workplace	**1.36**	

■ *Foreign Earnings Deduction* (seafarers only) **1.37** £

■ *Foreign tax for which tax credit relief not claimed* **1.38** £

Student Loans

■ *Student Loans repaid by deduction by employer* - see Notes, page EN8 **1.39** £

1.40 *Additional information*

Now fill in any other supplementary Pages that apply to you.
Otherwise, go back to page 2 in your Tax Return and finish filling it in.

BS 12/2001net   TAX RETURN ■ EMPLOYMENT: PAGE E2

Fig. 13. Page 2 of employment pages of self-assessment tax return.

However, you do not always have to claim this first year allowance if it is not beneficial.

The allowance works by claiming the allowance for the first year, then deducting the amount claimed, then the reduced amount is the basis for the next year's claim. This means that the claims can never exceed the cost of the asset. If the asset is sold there is a balancing charge or balancing allowance depending on the sale process.

Example

Cost of asset	5,000
First year allowance 50%	2,500
Written down value year 1	2,500
Allowance year 2 at 25% of £2,500	625
Written down value year 2	1,875
Allowance year 3 at 25% of £1,875	469
Written down value year 3	1,406
Sold for £1,300	1,300
Balancing allowance year 4	106

Thus the cost of the asset was £5,000, and it was sold in year 4 for £1,300. It has therefore had a net cost of £3,700. The capital allowances have been:

Year 1	2,500	
Year 2	625	
Year 3	469	
Year 4	106	
Total allowances		£3,700

If it had been sold for, say, £1,600, there would be an excess over the written down value, and a balancing charge would be made (ie the opposite of a balancing allowance) of £194, the excess proceeds received.

Pooling assets

For capital allowance purposes all your assets on which you claim capital allowances are put into one global figure – *except motor cars*. This is known as 'pooling'. It means that you do not have to calculate the allowances separately on each item and makes the calculations easier. When new items are added they are simply added to the pool, and when items are sold or scrapped they are deducted from the pool.

Example

Pool brought forward	40,000
Equipment sold	1,000
Balance of pool	39,000
Capital allowance for the year 25%	9,750
Balance carried forward	£29,250

When a new item is bought, and the first year allowance of 40% is claimed, that item is not put into the pool until the following year.

Example

Pool brought forward		40,000
New equipment bought	10,000	
First year allowance	4,000	
Balance carried forward	6,000	
Normal allowance on brought forward balance		10,000
Balance carried forward		30,000
Total carried forward to next year's pool		36,000
Total allowances claimed		£14,000

Special cases

Motor cars

As mentioned above, motor cars are not included in the general pool. Each car is calculated separately and has its own balance carried forward. There is no higher first year allowance for cars, and the normal allowance for any one year cannot exceed £3,000 for any one car.

Example

	Ford car	Vauxhall car	Rover car	
Balance brought forward	8,000	16,000		
Car sold	6,000			
Balancing allowance	2,000			
Car added			12,000	
Allowance claimed		(max) 3,000	3,000	
Balance carried forward		13,000	9,000	
Total allowance claimed				£8,000

Short-life assets

Where assets are not expected to have a long life they can be treated separately, in their own specific 'pool'. Examples could include vans or electronic equipment. This treatment is optional, but is often advantageous. The following example illustrates why this is so.

Example

You have a pool of expenditure brought forward of £30,000, and expenditure brought forward on short-life asset pool (a van) of £10,000. You sell the van from the short-life pool for £8,000, and buy a new van for £12,000. Compare the positions if all the assets were in the general pool:

	With separate short life assets pool		With one general pool
	Short-life assets	General pool	General pool
Balance brought forward	10,000	30,000	40,000

Van sold	8,000		8,000
Balancing allowance	2,000		
Subtotal			32,000
New van	12,000		12,000
Subtotal			44,000
First year allowance 40%	4,800		4,800
Normal allowance		7,500	8,000
Balance carried forward	7,200	22,500	31,200
Total allowance claimed		£14,300	£12,800

Is it always best to claim the first year allowance?

The answer to this is – not always. In some circumstances claiming the first year allowance in full can lead to a greater charge to tax. This typically happens when an asset has been written down to a relatively small figure, and then is sold at a higher figure than this written down value.

Example

You have a pool of expenditure brought forward of £10,000. You sell a machine for £30,000, and buy a new one for £45,000.

If you claimed the first year allowance in full the position would look like this:

Pool brought forward	10,000	
Proceeds of sale	30,000	
Balancing charge		20,000
New machine	45,000	
First year allowance 40%	18,000	
Balance carried forward	£27,000	

There has been a net charge to tax of £2,000, despite having spent £45,000 on new machinery.

If you do not claim the first year allowance the position would look like this:

60

Pool brought forward	10,000
New machine	45,000
	55,000
Proceeds of sale	30,000
	25,000
Normal allowance 25%	6,250
Balance carried forward	£18,750

This time there has been a net allowance against tax of £6,250 instead of a charge of £2,000!

But you could do even better than this, because the first year does not have to be either claimed or disclaimed in full. You can disclaim part only of the first year allowance. So the position could then look like this:

Pool brought forward		10,000	
New machine	45,000		
Less partial claim	20,000	20,000	(partial disclaim added to pool)
	25,000		
First year allowance 40%	10,000		
Subtotal of pool value		30,000	
Proceeds of sale		30,000	
Balancing figure		Nil	
Balance carried forward	£15,000		

In this case there has been an allowance against tax of £10,000.

Of course the thing to remember is that as more of the allowance is claimed in the current year, there is less to carry forward to future years.

Disclaiming capital allowances

Tax tip
Capital allowances do not have to be claimed in their

entirety. You have the right not to claim the allowances, or to restrict the claim. This could be advantageous if your income is already not enough to make you taxable even before the allowances.

Example
You are a married person and have business profits of £4,800. You can claim capital allowances on assets with a value of £3,000.

	If you claimed full allowances	If you restricted your claim
Profits	4,800	4,800
Capital allowances	750	185
Net amount	4,050	4,615
Personal allowance	4,615	4,615
Taxable	Nil	Nil
Capital expenditure carried forward	£2,250	£2,815

Thus although there is no difference in the nil tax liability, you have more to carry forward and claim for capital allowances in future years.

How do you restrict your claim?
Work out the restricted amount of allowances you wish to claim, then enter the amounts in box 1.35 of the employment pages (see Figure 13), or boxes 3.14 to 3.23 of the self-employment pages (see Figure 14) of your self-assessment tax return.

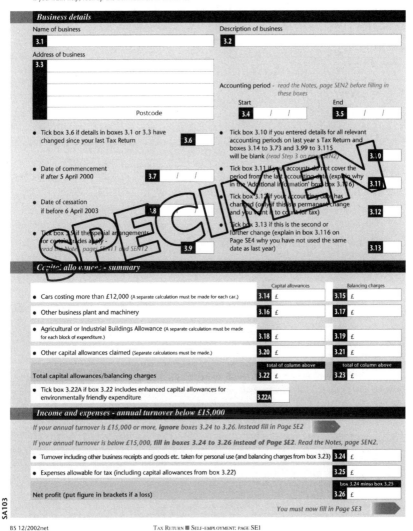

Fig. 14. Page 1 of self-employment pages of self-assessment tax return.

63

USING YOUR RELIEFS

Reliefs are given in a different way from allowances. Generally they are recognition of payments or expenses of some sort which are allowed as deductions from your income for tax purposes. These reliefs have to be claimed on your tax return, therefore make sure you claim all the reliefs to which you are entitled.

How do you claim reliefs?
Claim reliefs by entering the details on page 5 of your self-assessment tax return (see Figure 4).

Pension contributions

You are allowed to claim relief against your income in respect of premiums you pay towards **retirement schemes**. However, in order to qualify for the tax relief the retirement scheme has to be recognised by the Inland Revenue, and the rules of the scheme have to comply with Inland Revenue requirements. Further details of the tax reliefs and the schemes are given in Chapter 14.

How do you claim relief for pension contributions?
Enter details in boxes 14.1 to 14.11 on page 5 of your self-assessment tax return (see Figure 4). Payments under retirement annuity contracts are still paid gross, and the tax relief is obtained by entering the amounts in boxes 14.1 to 14.5, including payments carried back to the previous year and payments brought back from the following year. Payments under personal pension schemes and stakeholder schemes already have basic rate tax deducted at source. Relief is given for the higher rates of tax (if any) by entering the details in boxes 14.6 to 14.11.

Interest on loans

You can claim tax relief at your highest marginal rate of tax on interest on the following types of loans:

- A loan to invest money in a partnership in which you are a partner, or in a limited company in which you are a director.

- A loan to buy land or property which is used by a partnership in which you are a partner.

- A loan to buy plant or machinery for use in a business of a partnership in which you are a partner.

- A loan to pay inheritance tax.

How do you claim loan interest?
Enter details in box 15.1 on page 5 of your self-assessment tax return (see Figure 4).

Maintenance or alimony

Since 14 March 1988 tax relief can be claimed on certain payments of **maintenance** or **alimony**. The payments must be made under a court order or a written agreement under an assessment made under the Child Support Act 1991. The tax relief is the lower of:

- the amount of maintenance or alimony paid, and the married couple's tax allowance for the year, as it was before being abolished for people under 65.

How do you claim maintenance or alimony?
Enter details in box 15.2 and 15.2a on page 5 of your self-assessment tax return (see Figure 4).

Venture Capital Trusts

Venture Capital Trusts are investments in businesses not quoted on the Stock Exchange, which meet certain criteria. Investments up to £100,000 attract tax relief up front of 20%. There are also other Capital Gains Tax advantages in Venture Capital Trusts.

How do you claim relief for investments in Venture Capital Trusts?
Enter details in box 15.3 on page 5 of your self-assessment tax return (see Figure 4).

Enterprise Investment Scheme

The **Enterprise Investment Scheme** is similar to the Venture Capital Trusts. Tax relief at 20% is given on investments in shares in qualifying companies, with an upper limit of £150,000. This scheme also has similar Capital Gains Tax advantages to the Venture Capital Trusts.

How do you claim relief for investments in Enterprise Investment Schemes?
Enter details in box 15.4 on page 5 of your self-assessment tax return (see Figure 4).

Gift Aid

If you make any payment to a registered charity you may sign a **Gift Aid** form, which the charity can provide, and the amount is deemed to be net of basic rate income tax. The charity can then claim back the deemed tax.

How do you claim for Gift Aid payments?
Enter details in boxes 15A.1 to 15A.5 on page 6 of your self-assessment tax return (see Figure 5).

Community investment

If you have invested money in a Community Development Finance Institution, this may fall within the tax credit scheme, and you may therefore be able to claim tax relief for this investment.

The following are the conditions for claiming this tax relief:

- the investment must have been made after 17 April 2002, and
- the institution must have issued a tax relief certificate, and
- the investment must be retained for at least five years.

The tax relief available is the lower of:

- 5% of the original investment for each year that the investment is held, and that the relief is available, or
- the amount that reduces your tax liability to zero for that year.

How do you claim relief for Community Investment?
Enter details in boxes 15.5 to 15.7 on page 5 of your self-assessment tax return (see Figure 4). NB: Box 15.5 is for claiming relief for a preceding year, and cannot be used in the 2002/2003 tax return, since 2002/2003 was the first year the relief was available.

Post-cessation expenses

If you have ceased a business and then incurred expenses relating to the business after that date, or incurred a bad debt of the business after that date, you may be able to claim tax relief in the year you incur those expenses. The payments must be made within seven years of the cessation of the business.

> **How do you claim relief for post-cessation expenses?** Enter the details in box 15.8 on page 5 of your self-assessment tax return (see Figure 4).

Annuities and annual payments (covenants)

If you are a higher rate tax payer, you may be able to claim tax relief on the higher rate tax liability for payments made under annuities and covenants if they were entered into for full value and for genuine commercial reasons in connection with your trade or profession. These payments are treated as if paid after basic rate tax has been deducted.

> **How do you claim relief for annuities and annual payments?** Enter the details (only the actual amount paid, not the tax treated as if it were deducted) in box 15.9 on page 5 of your self-assessment tax return (see Figure 4).

Payments to a trade union or friendly society for death benefit

If you pay:

- subscriptions to a trade union, which include benefits for a pension, life assurance or funeral benefits, or
- premiums to a friendly society which combines sickness and death benefits, if:
  - the total premium is no more than £25 per month, and
  - no more than 40% of the premium is charged for the death benefit,

  then one half of the amount paid for the allowable benefit is given as relief.

> **How do you claim relief for these payments?**
> Enter one half of the amount paid for the allowable benefit in box 15.10 on page 5 of your self-assessment tax return (see Figure 4).

Payments under an employer's compulsory widow's, widower's or orphan's benefit scheme

Payments made under such schemes which are compulsory under the contract of employment (or by Act of Parliament) may allow tax relief. Relief is normally given under the PAYE system, and no claim is necessary here. However, in some situations, relief is not given under the PAYE system, and must be claimed here.

> **How do you claim relief under these schemes?**
> Enter the details of any amount not relieved under PAYE in box 15.11 on page 5 of your self-assessment tax return (see Figure 4). NB: £100 is the maximum that can be relieved in this way.

Qualifying distribution on the redemption of bonus shares or distributions

You may have received bonus shares (or other securities), and these have subsequently been redeemed. This redemption payment will have carried a tax credit, and will have been declared as dividend income on page three of the self-assessment tax return. If you are liable to tax at the higher rate, the higher rate tax payable or paid on the issue of those bonus shares or securities will have been taxed twice, and can therefore be relieved.

> **How do you claim relief for redemption of bonus shares?**
> Enter the upper dividend rate tax paid in box 15.12 on page 5 of your self-assessment tax return (see Figure 4).

USING YOUR LOWER RATE TAX BANDS

An 'allowance'

You can look on your lower rate tax bands as a sort of allowance. If you are married and have some control over income you can ensure that your allowances and your family's allowances are fully used up. You can also make sure that the lower rate bands are used up as much as possible.

For instance, if the husband is taxable at 40%, but the wife is only taxable at 10%, it would make sense to transfer some of the income to the wife and thereby save 30% on the income transferred. The same is true, of course, if one partner is taxable at 40% and the other at 22%, or one at 22% and the other at 10%.

Example

Mr and Mrs Jones have the following income and tax liability:

	Husband	*Wife*
Salary	35,000	5,000
Interest	3,000	1,000
Total income	£38,000	£6,000
Personal allowance	4,615	4,615
Taxable	£33,385	£1,385

Tax due:	Husband	Wife
10% × £1,960	196.00	
10% × £1,385		138.50
20% × £3,000 (interest)	600.00	
22% × £25,540	5,618.80	
40% × £2,885	1,154.00	
Net tax liabilities	£7,568.80	£138.50

The total tax paid between them is £7,707.30.

If they transferred the source of interest from the husband to the wife the result would be:

Salary	35,000	5,000
Interest		4,000
	35,000	9,000
Personal allowance	4,615	4,615
Taxable	£30,385	£4,385
Tax due: 10% × £1,960	196.00	196.00
20% × £2,425 (interest)		485.00
22% × £28,425	6,253.50	
Net tax liabilities	£6,449.50	£681.00

The total tax paid between them is £7,130.50

There has been a saving of £576.80, by using up the wife's lower rate tax band to the full.

How do you use up lower rate bands?
Use up lower rate bands by ensuring that income is divided between husband and wife in the right proportions. It is simple to transfer a building society account or bank account to your spouse's name. He or she opens up a new account, and you withdraw the right amount and give it to him or her. Shares or unit trusts can be transferred by writing to the company or unit trust manager. They will send you transfer forms to sign.

USING OVERLAP RELIEF

At the same time as self-assessment was introduced, the basis of assessment for partners and self-employed people (Schedule D) changed. Previously it was on the 'preceding year basis' (ie the profits of the accounting year ending in one tax year were taxed in the next tax year). The new basis, currently in use, is the 'current year basis'. This means that the profits of the accounting year ending in a tax year are taxed in that same year.

There are special rules for calculating the opening years' assessments for a new business, and the closing years when a business finishes. The overall effect is that the exact amount of profits made in the life of a business is assessed to tax. (Under the old system when it was possible for the amount assessed to tax to be different from the amount of profits in the life of the business.) This works by way of calculating overlap profits.

Overlap relief is a means of giving relief where part of the profits of a business are assessed to tax twice. This can happen in two ways:

1. The calculations for the assessment of profits in the opening years of a new business can mean that part of the profits are taxed twice. This depends on the timing of the start of the new business, and the accounting date used. (In general, if 31 March or 5 April are used as the accounting date, there will not be any 'double taxing'.)

2. Businesses which were in existence before the change to the 'current year' basis and continued afterwards had special rules for assessing the profits in the three-year transition period. This could also give rise to some profits being assessed twice, and overlap relief could be claimed.

This overlap relief is not given straight away, but it is carried forward. It can only be used:

- when the business ceases
- or when there is a change of accounting date.

How do you claim overlap relief?

First, enter the amount of overlap profit worked out as above, in box 3.78 on page 3 of the self-employed pages (see Figure 17), or in box 4.9 on page 1 of the partnership pages (see Figure 18).

Then when it is used, enter the amount used in box 3.79 (for self-employed people on their own) or box 4.10 (for self-employed people in partnership). In any year, if you do not claim the overlap relief it is carried forward, and you should enter the overlap relief carried forward in box 3.80 (for self-employed people on their own) or box 4.11 (for self-employed people in partnership).

Tax tip

Do not forget to enter the amount brought forward from the previous year's tax return, then carry it forward to the next one. This way you will not lose sight of the relief and forget to claim it.

If the overlap can only be used in these two circumstances, think carefully about the ways in which you could use it.

The cessation of business rules can happen:

- when the business finishes for good
- or when the business changes format, for example a sole trader takes on a partner, or vice versa, or when a sole trader or partnership decides to become a limited company.

Obviously it is not a good strategy to cease business permanently just to make use of the overlap relief. But if you are thinking of changing the format it could be advantageous to think about the timing, particularly if there is a year when profits are high and you may be taxed at the higher rate.

Tax tip
It may be possible, if the timing is right, to get the relief at 40%, although the original overlap profits were only taxed at the basic rate or even the lower rate.

The other circumstance in which you can use the overlap relief is a change of accounting date. This is something over which you have full control. It may well be worthwhile to change your accounting date:

- if you have high profits which will put you into the higher rate of tax, and
- there is sufficient overlap relief brought forward.

TAX EFFICIENCY AUDIT

1. Are you and your family using all the allowances to which you are entitled?

2. Are you able to avoid entering the higher marginal rate of tax?

3. Are you claiming all the reliefs to which you are entitled?

4. Is there anything on which you could claim capital allowances?

5. Do you need to claim capital allowances in full?

6. Are you able to use overlap relief by changing your accounting period or by changing the format of your business?

4

Concessions and Special Cases

TIMING YOUR TRANSACTIONS

If you have control over your income, or some parts of it, you may be able to control the timing of receipt of the income. This could be useful in saving tax. There may, for instance, be occasions when you know you will be paying less tax one year than in the following or the preceding year. The tax rates and the personal allowances usually alter from one year to another, and it may be useful to have income in a later year to benefit from the higher allowances or lower rates of tax in the later year.

Another scenario in which your tax liability could change drastically from one year to the next is on retirement. You could well be paying the top rate of tax the year before you retire, then the basic or even the lower rate after you retire. This could be partly due to the drop in your income, and partly due to the extra tax allowance on reaching the age of 65. There is a further increase in the allowance (though not so great) on reaching age 75.

Another reason for postponing income from one year to the next is that there is a further year in which to pay the tax. For instance, income received on 5 April 2001 will suffer tax payable on 31 January 2002. Income received on 6th April 2001 will suffer tax payable on 31 January 2003.

Bringing income forward

How can you bring income forward?
If you wish to have income taxed in a current year instead of the next tax year, and you have a bank or building society account or some other form of money on deposit, you could close the account.

This could help if the interest would have been payable in, say, June. By closing the account in March the interest is then paid up to the date of closing the account, and therefore comes before 5 April. Of course, you must be certain that there is no penalty on closing the account and that you can get at least as good an interest rate in a new account.

Postponing income

How can you postpone income?
You may also be able to use a bank or building society account to postpone income. This is only possible where the right sort of account exists. There are long-term accounts (such as five years) which only pay interest at the end of the five years. Some such accounts are promoted by some building societies in the form of 'Stockmarket Bonds'. They guarantee to pay an interest rate which at least matches the increase in the Stockmarket index over a five-year period. The interest for the whole five years is then paid at the end of the term. This does produce a bunching of five years' interest all receivable in one year, but it does also postpone income.

Accrued income
Certain fixed interest securities, such as government stocks,

pay interest half-yearly. If you buy or sell them on the Stock Exchange an adjustment is made on the price to account for interest accrued from the last interest payment. Thus, if you are buying, you have to pay extra for the interest accrued since the last payment. This is because you will receive the whole of the next half-yearly interest payment. It works the opposite way round if you are selling.

Thus you can either be paying for accrued interest, or receiving accrued interest. If you receive it you are taxable on it, and if you pay it you can deduct it from the interest you receive. This arrangement does allow a certain amount of flexibility in timing the transactions. It could put income into a different tax year. However, you must bear in mind that doing this will incur dealing costs. It is therefore not something to be recommended to carry out on a regular basis, but to bear in mind as a one-off way of influencing the timing of income.

This is a general principle, since the opportunities to save tax by timing tend to occur infrequently. We have already seen the sort of occasions on which this can be useful, such as:

- retirement
- attaining the age of 65, or 75
- receiving an abnormal income or profit which puts you in the higher rate tax band for one year only.

Question
I expect my business to take off next year, and earn really big profits. Should I put off paying a pension premium so that I can claim it later when I expect to be in higher rates of tax?

Answer
It all depends on how concrete your expectations are. We all tend to be over-optimistic about our business prospects in

the future. I would caution against putting off pension premiums for too long. The effect of postponing premiums to a pension policy can be far more drastic to the end result than the tax benefit. If there is any doubt, continue to pay a modest amount now – one that you can comfortably afford. Then put in more when your business does better and you can better afford extra premiums.

EXTRA STATUTORY CONCESSIONS AND SPECIAL CASES

The Inland Revenue publish concessions. These are treatments of certain items for tax purposes which are not laid down by law, but allowed by the Inland Revenue. They are all treatments which benefit the taxpayer. The list of concessions is long, and it is not possible to give an exhaustive one here, but here are some of the concessions which you may find useful:

- Flat rate expenses for tools, clothing etc. These are allowances agreed for employees in various trades or industry groups. They are usually agreed with the relevant trades unions. Check with your union or employer to see if there is a claim you can make.

> **How do you claim flat rate expenses?**
> When you have found out the amount enter it in your self-assessment tax return box 1.33 on page 2 of the employment pages (see Figure 13).

- Luncheon vouchers given by employers are not taxable up to certain limits.

- Travel expenses from home to work are not normally allowable against tax. But if an employer reimburses

78

travel costs for home to work travel, that can be free of tax if it is as a result of public transport disruption due to industrial action, or by severely disabled employees unable to use public transport.

• Arrears of tax due to official error. If the Inland Revenue have not charged you tax, even though you have given them all the information, and then they charge you late, you may apply for some or all of the tax to be remitted. The level of remission depends on your total income in the year of notification of the tax arrears, as follows:

Taxpayer's gross income	Tax remitted
up to £15,500	all
£15,501 to £18,000	three quarters
£18,001 to £22,000	one half
£22,001 to £26,000	one quarter
£26,001 to £40,000	one tenth
Over £40,000	none

How can you get this remission of tax?
If you have been in these circumstances, make sure you claim the exemption by demanding it from your Tax Inspector.

• If your employer has a suggestions scheme to which all employees are able to contribute, and you gain an award (up to £5,000), it is not taxable by concession.

• Long service awards of tangible goods, or shares in the employer company, to people who have served for at least 20 years with the same employer are not taxable by concession provided that the cost to the employer does not exceed £20 for each year of service, and no similar award has been made in the previous ten years to the same person.

- Capital allowances. If you cease a business you may use capital allowances brought forward to reduce the profit or create a loss for the final year's assessment.

- Overseas employment. Certain lump sums from termination of overseas employment may not be taxable.

GETTING THE RIGHT TAX CREDITS

Since 6 April 1999, dividends from companies have carried a tax credit of 10% (previously the figure was 20%). Further, this tax credit had always been repayable in the past, but is no longer.

Taxpayers who pay tax at either the lower, or the basic rate, incur no further liability. Higher rate taxpayers are liable to the extra tax charge for the higher rate. However, those who would otherwise have been due for a repayment, because their personal allowances have not been fully used, are not able to reclaim the tax credit on dividends. If you are in this position, you should think about changing your investment from shares which attract dividends to interest which is either paid gross, or with tax deducted at source. This tax deducted at source will still be repayable.

Before you resort to this, however, stop to think about your investment objectives and whether a change from shares to interest bearing loans will continue to meet those objectives.

GETTING TAX RELIEF ON TRAVELLING EXPENSES

If you are employed the normal rule about tax relief on travel expenses is that home to work travel (what we shall call 'commuting') is not allowable. However, this applies to travel between your home and your permanent workplace. A 'permanent workplace' is one which the employee *expects* to attend regularly:

- for more than 24 months

- or for the whole period he holds that particular employment.

Note the word in italics, it is very important.

Certain employees, in particular site-based ones, do not fit into this pattern. Their workplace shifts as the employer's work demands alter. This is most common for building site employees, and computer programmers or analysts, who frequently get sent to different locations for their work.

If you are in this position, and you are working at different sites for 24 months or less, then make sure you claim your travel expenses.

There is another twist to the claim, however. This concerns the emphasised word above. If you have an assignment which you expect to be less than two years, you can claim your travel expenses. However, if you are then informed, say, 20 months into the assignment that it is to be extended, your expectation is now that the assignment will last more than 24 months, so you are not eligible any more to claim travel expenses.

Not all assignments fit neatly into this pattern, however. Your job might entail going to a main office or factory most of the time, and a few days a month at another location. It is possible under the rules to have more than one permanent workplace. However, a workplace is not permanent if:

- it does not last more than 24 months

- or it takes less than 40% of the employee's working time.

Tax tip
If you are in any borderline case try to arrange with your employer that the assignment will be either:

- 24 months or less
- or less than 40% of your total working time.

How do you arrange this?
You will have to be dependent on your employer for this scheme. It is better to have the terms written into a contract. It is possible that the Inspector of Taxes would challenge this, and any form of written evidence will help your case. Claim the expenses by completing box 1.32 on page 2 of the employment pages of your self-assessment tax return (see Figure 13).

If you are an employer you could try to arrange this for your employees, and make sure they are aware they can claim their travel expenses. They will probably be very happy about it.

CAR BENEFITS

If you have the use of a company car, the benefit assessed for tax is based on a combination of the car's list price and its carbon dioxide emissions. All makes and models of car first registered since 1 January 1998 have an official rating for carbon dioxide emissions.

The assessment is calculated as a percentage of the car's list price, those percentages calculated in accordance with the carbon dioxide emissions. The benefit figure covers the whole benefit for the use of the car except provision of a chaffeur, which is assessed separately.

The list price is:

- The price on the day before the first registration of the vehicle.
- Inclusive of VAT.

- Subject to an upper limit of £80,000.
- Includes accessories.
- Reduced by the employee's contribution to the cost of the car, when it is first made available (subject to a maximum deduction of £5,000).

The percentage to be used is obtained from the table shown in Figure 15. The benefit is then reduced:

- by any contribution made by the employee, and
- proportionately if the car is not available for the whole year, and
- if the car is incapable of being used for 30 consecutive days or more.

Special cases

Older cars

If the car was first registered before 1 January 1998, the following percentages are applied to the list price as above:

Engine size	Percentage
Up to 1400cc	15%
1401–2000cc	22%
Over 2000cc	32%

Cars for which there is no authorised carbon dioxide emissions figure

If the car has no authorised carbon dioxide emissions figure, the following percentages are applied to the list price as above:

Engine size	Percentage
Up to 1400cc	15%
1401–2000cc	25%
Over 2000cc	35%

If the engine is diesel powered, the percentages are increased by 3%, but cannot exceed 35%.

Vintage cars
If the car is more than 15 years old, the open market value is used if more than the list price of the car.

Vans
If the vehicle provided is not a car but a van, the following benefits apply (i.e. not related to list price or percentage):

Age of van	*Benefit*
Under 4 years old at the end of tax year	£500
4 years old and over at the end of tax year	£350

If the van is not provided for the whole year, or if it is unavailable for 30 consecutive days or more, there is a proportionate reduction. Where one van is provided to more than one employee, the charge is divided equally between the employees who use the van, irrespective of the variations in their private use. If an employee has the use of the van for only part of the year, his shared profit is not reduced proportionately. An employee may claim to be taxed on £5 per day of private use instead of the normal shared calculation, if it is beneficial.

NB: This benefit includes the use of the van and fuel for private use.

Car fuel charge
If car fuel is provided for private use, the benefit is assessed for tax. The benefit is reduced to nil if the employee bears the cost of *all* fuel for private use, or pays for it himself. Apart from this there is no reduction.

Carbon dioxide emissions in grams per kilometre			Percentage of list price taxable
2002/2003	*2003/2004*	*2004/2005*	
165	155	145	15%
170	160	150	16%
175	165	155	17%
180	170	160	18%
185	175	165	19%
190	180	170	20%
195	185	175	21%
200	190	180	22%
205	195	185	23%
210	200	190	24%
215	205	195	25%
220	210	200	26%
225	215	205	27%
230	220	210	28%
235	225	215	29%
240	230	220	30%
245	235	225	31%
250	240	230	32%
255	245	235	33%
260	250	240	34%
265	255	245	35%

If the car runs solely on diesel, the percentages are increased by 3, but up to a maximum of 35%.

Figure 15. Table of percentages of list price of cars to be applied for car benefit.

Warning
There is no benefit from the employee bearing *part* of the cost of fuel for private use. The whole of the fuel benefit is still charged.

The car fuel benefit is calculated at a percentage of a fixed figure, which for 2003/2004 is £14,400. The percentage is the same as that shown in Figure 15.

Mileage and fuel rates

If an employee uses their own car for business use, the approved rate for reimbursement by the employer is 40p per mile for the first 10,000 miles per year, and 25p per mile thereafter.

Advisory rates for reimbursement for fuel of private mileage by employees, or employer's reimbursement for fuel for business mileage are as follows:

Engine size	Petrol	Diesel	LPG
Up to 1400cc	10p	9p	6p
1401–2000cc	12p	9p	7p
Over 2000cc	14p	12p	9p

Any reimbursements up to the above figures will be accepted by the Inland Revenue as not giving rise to any taxable benefit.

Saving tax

Tax can be reduced by having a company van instead of a car. However, this may not always be desirable or possible. An alternative may be to buy the car personally, and charge the employer for its use on company business, using the statutory rates.

There can be no general rule to calculate the most tax efficient method – each case must be calculated on its own merits and the actual figures involved.

It could also be benefical to explore the use of alternatively fuelled cars.

> **How do you know what to enter on your tax return for car benefit?**
> Your employer will have some means of checking the figure. After the end of the tax year the employer will issue you with a copy of the P11D return they have made relating to you. You should then enter these amounts on page 1 of the employment pages with your self-assessment tax return (see Figure 16).

USING LOSSES

Using trading losses

Even the best run businesses can sometimes make a loss due to circumstances beyond their control. The one compensation is that losses can be used to reduce tax. There are seven main ways in which trading losses can be used:

- By set-off against other income of the same year, or of the preceding year. You can claim a trading loss as a reduction of your income in either of these years.

- By carry-forward against future profits of the same trade.

- By carry-back of losses in the first four years of assessment of a new trade. The losses may be carried back and offset against any income of the three preceding years.

- By carry-back of the losses incurred in the 12 months leading up to a permanent discontinuance of a trade. These losses are allowed against profits from the same trade in the three preceding years.

- By setting off trading losses against capital gains in the same year.

- By carrying forward losses from a business which is transferred to a limited company to offset against future income derived from that company, including salary and dividends.

- By claiming post-cessation expenses as a loss in the year in which they are incurred. There may be expenses incurred after a business has ceased, relating to that business, and these can be claimed as a loss in the same year. This is only available up to seven years from the cessation of business.

Deciding which relief to claim

If you make a business loss you should decide which is the best way to claim to gain the best tax advantage.

First, of course, you must work out which reliefs are available – there may be more than one option. So ask yourself if the loss was made in the early years of a business, or the closing year, or after cessation.

Next, work out which tax years would be available for claiming the loss. It could be up to three years back, or indefinitely carried forward.

Then work out what your top rate of tax was in each of those years, and how much of your income was taxed at that top rate. In the case of carrying losses forward you may have to make an estimate of what profits you expect to be making in the next tax years.

Then make the appropriate claim.

However, remember the wrinkles:

- There are time limits for making loss claims. Make sure you make the claim within the time limit. Generally the time limit is 12 months after 31 January following the end of the year of assessment.

Inland Revenue

Name   **Tax reference**

Fill in these boxes first

If you want help, look up the box numbers in the Notes.

Details of employer

Employer's PAYE reference - may be shown under 'Inland Revenue office number and reference' on your P60 or 'PAYE reference' on your P45

1.1

Employer's name

1.2

Date employment started
(only if between 6 April 2002 and 5 April 2003)

1.3 /   /

Employer's address

1.5

Date employment finished
(only if between 6 April 2002 and 5 April 2003)

1.4 /   /

Tick box 1.6 if you were a director of the company

1.6

and, if so, tick box 1.7 if it was a close company

1.7

Postcode

Income from employment

■ **Money** - *see Notes, page EN3*

Before tax

- Payments from P60 (or P45) **1.8** £

- Payments not on P60, etc. **1.9** £

  - other payments (excluding expenses entered below and lump sums and compensation payments or benefits entered overleaf) **1.10** £

Tax deducted

- Tax deducted in the UK from payments in boxes 1.8 to 1.10 **1.11** £

■ **Benefits and expenses** - *see Notes, pages EN3 to EN6. If any benefits connected with termination of employment were received, or enjoyed, after that termination and were from a former employer you need to complete Help Sheet IR204, available from the Orderline. Do not enter such benefits here.*

	Amount			Amount
• Assets transferred/ payments made for you	**1.12** £		• Vans	**1.18** £
• Vouchers, credit cards and tokens	**1.13** £		• Interest-free and low-interest loans *see Note for box 1.19, page EN5*	**1.19** £
• Living accommodation	**1.14** £		*box 1.20 is not used*	
• Excess mileage allowances and passenger payments	**1.15** £		• Private medical or dental insurance	**1.21** £
• Company cars	**1.16** £		• Other benefits	**1.22** £
• Fuel for company cars	**1.17** £		• Expenses payments received and balancing charges	**1.23** £

SA101

Fig. 16. Page 1 of employment pages of self-assessment tax return.

89

- Remember that if you make a claim to relate the losses back to previous tax years, there could well be extra interest added on to any repayment of tax. This could well tip the balance in favour of making a claim to throw losses back.

Tax tip
Remember that capital allowances can be used to increase a loss, or indeed to create a loss. Also, capital allowances do not have to be claimed in full. If a loss cannot be used fully, you could reduce or disclaim capital allowances.

How do you make a claim for losses?
Make a claim for loss relief on your self-assessment tax return – in boxes 3.85 to 3.89 on page 3 of the self-employment pages (see Figure 17) or boxes 4.14 to 4.20 on page 1 of the partnership pages if you are in a partnership (see Figure 18).

Question
Is it worth deliberately manufacturing a loss to get the tax relief?

Answer
Making a loss is not really something you can or should do 'at will'. You can only make use of a loss when it has genuinely occurred in your business. The advice about this is similar to the advice about expenses. You are worse off when you make a loss, even after the tax relief. However, one thing you can do is to create or increase a loss by claiming capital allowances. Consider the following set of circumstances.

Tax tip
If your business is a limited company, losses may be carried back to the previous year and offset against Corporation Tax paid then.

Example
Supposing your company made a profit of £25,000 the previous year on which it paid Corporation Tax of £4,375. For the current year you have a break even situation (no profit and no loss). If you vote yourself as director a bonus of £25,000, this creates a loss to throw back to the previous year, and get a repayment of the Corporation Tax. The tax (and National Insurance) cost of the bonus is offset by the refund of Corporation Tax, which can make it worthwhile.

IS IT WORTH BECOMING A TAX EXILE?

Living abroad has a romantic ring about it, conjuring up glamorous visions of an idyllic lifestyle on a tropical beach alongside film stars and pop stars. What is the reality behind it?

Weighing up the pros and cons
Even if your income is such that you are seriously considering becoming a tax exile, there are other, non-financial matters to bear in mind. You must become resigned, above all, to not being able to be in the UK for certain times. You may not be able to plan all the occasions when you would like to return to this country. There may be unforeseen events, family crises or other events.

Quite apart from the patriotic aspect, there is the simple matter of having to monitor your movements. You must be quite sure that you will be happy living in the country of your choice. Many people enjoy the initial 'honeymoon' period, but disillusionment settles in after a while. And, of

You **must** fill in boxes 3.74 and 3.75 and **all other boxes** that apply to you, on this Page

Adjustments to arrive at taxable profit or loss

Basis period begins **3.74** / /   and ends **3.75** / /

Profit or loss of this account for tax purposes (box 3.26 or 3.73)   **3.76** £

Adjustment to arrive at profit or loss for this basis period   **3.77** £

- Overlap profit brought forward **3.78** £   • Deduct overlap relief used this year **3.79** £

- Overlap profit carried forward **3.80** £

Averaging for farmers and creators of literary or artistic works (see Notes, page SEN8, if you made a loss for 2001-02)   **3.81** £

Adjustment on change of basis   **3.82** £

Net profit for 2001-02 (if you made a loss, enter '0')   **3.83** £

Allowable loss for 2001-02 (if you made a profit, enter '0')   **3.84** £

- Loss offset against other income for 2001-02   **3.85** £

- Loss to carry back   **3.86** £

- Loss to carry forward
  (that is allowable loss not claimed in any other way)   **3.87** £

- Losses brought forward from earlier years   **3.88** £

- Losses brought forward from earlier years used this year   **3.89** £

box 3.83 minus box 3.89
Taxable profit after losses brought forward   **3.90** £

- Any other business income (for example, Business Start-up Allowance received in 2001-02)   **3.91** £

box 3.90 + box 3.91
Total taxable profits from this business   **3.92** £

- Tick box 3.93 if the figure in box 3.92 is provisional   **3.93**

Class 4 National Insurance contributions

- Tick box 3.94 if exception or deferment applies   **3.94**

- Adjustments to profit chargeable to Class 4 National Insurance contributions   **3.95** £

Class 4 National Insurance contributions due   **3.96** £

Subcontractors in the construction industry

- Deductions made by contractors on account of tax (you must send your CIS25s to us)   **3.97** £

Tax deducted from trading income

- Any tax deducted (excluding deductions made by contractors on account of tax) from trading income   **3.98** £

Fig. 17. Page 3 of self-employment pages of self-assessment tax return.

Inland **Revenue**

Name

Tax reference

Fill in these boxes first

If you want help, look up the box numbers in the Notes

Partnership details

Partnership reference number | Description of partnership trade or profession

4.1 | **4.2**

- Date you started being a partner (if during 2002-03) **4.3** / /
- Date you stopped being a partner (if during 2002-03) **4.4** / /

Your share of the partnership's trading or professional income

Basis period begins **4.5** / / and ends **4.6** / /

- Your share of the profit or loss of this year's account for tax purposes (enter a loss in brackets) **4.7** £
- Adjustment to arrive at profit or loss for this basis period **4.8** £
- Overlap profit brought forward **4.9** £   Deduct overlap relief used this year **4.10** £
- Overlap profit carried forward **4.11** £
- Averaging for farmers and creators of literary or artistic works (see Notes, page PN3) if the partnership made a loss in 2002-03 foreign tax deducted, if tax credit relief not claimed **4.12** £
- Adjustment on change of basis **4.12A** £

Net profit for 2002-03 (if loss, enter '0' in box 4.13 and enter the loss in box 4.14) **4.13** £

Allowable loss for 2002-03 **4.14** £

- Loss offset against other income for 2002-03 **4.15** £
- Loss to carry back **4.16** £
- Loss to carry forward (that is, allowable loss not claimed in any other way) **4.17** £
- Losses brought forward from last year **4.18** £
- Losses brought forward from last year used this year **4.19** £

Taxable profit after losses brought forward   box 4.13 *minus* box 4.19 **4.20** £

- Add amounts **not** included in the partnership accounts that are needed to calculate your taxable profit (for example, Enterprise Allowance (Business Start-up Allowance) received in 2002-03) **4.21** £

Total taxable profits from this business   box 4.20 + box 4.21 **4.22** £

Class 4 National Insurance contributions

- Tick this box if exception or deferment applies **4.23**
- Adjustments to profit chargeable to Class 4 National Insurance contributions **4.24** £

Class 4 National Insurance contributions due **4.25** £

SA104

Fig. 18. Page 1 of partnership pages of self-assessment tax return.

93

course, you need to be sure that you will not be taxed more heavily in the country to which you go.

The basic rules
The basic rules are:

- If you are resident in the UK for any tax year you are liable to UK tax on all of your income and gains whether they are from UK or overseas sources.

- If you are non-resident in the UK you are only liable to income from sources in the UK.

- If you are not domiciled in the UK, but you are resident in the UK, you are liable to tax on overseas income only to the extent that it is remitted to the UK.

- If you are resident in the UK but not ordinarily resident, then you are only liable to UK tax on income remitted to this country.

Understanding the concepts
Your tax liability in this country may be dependent on your **residence**, your **ordinary residence**, or your **domicile**. You may be resident in this country, but not domiciled in this country. You may be resident but not ordinarily resident. You may even be resident in more than one country for tax purposes.

Residence
Strangely, there is very little actual statutory guidance on the definition of residence in the tax laws of this country. The concept of residence is largely one of actual physical presence in this country. When you are resident in this country for six months or more during a tax year, then you are resident for tax purposes.

If you leave this country to work abroad full time, you are

treated as non-resident, so long as the following conditions are met (and the Inland Revenue have indicated that they will accept that a self-employed business person working abroad meeting similar conditions is also non-resident):

- You must not visit this country for more than 182 days in the tax year.

- Your visits to this country averaged over four years do not exceed an average of 90 days per year.

- You must be working full time abroad under a contract of employment (not necessarily with an overseas company).

- You must be abroad (apart from the visits to this country) for the whole of the tax year concerned. Thus, you cannot be considered non-resident if you were abroad from 1 July to 30 June the following year. There is no full tax year involved here. (The tax year, of course, runs from 6 April to the following 5 April.)

If you leave the country permanently you are treated as non-resident if you do not visit this country for more than 90 days each year. If you retain accommodation in this country, you must produce evidence of some sort that your emigration from this country is permanent. Steps taken to acquire a permanent home abroad are the most convincing evidence.

Ordinary residence

This term is not defined anywhere in the tax laws of this country. It signifies a greater permanence, and is normally decided by habitual residence. You will normally be regarded as ordinarily resident if:

- you visit this country regularly, and

- you have accommodation available in this country, or

- your visits average more than 90 days per year (ignoring days in this country for circumstances beyond your control, such as illness of yourself or a family member).

Domicile
This is a different concept from residence. It is the country you consider as your permanent home. You acquire a domicile of origin at birth (normally the domicile of your father). You may then change this to a domicile of choice, determined by your subsequent actions, including marriage and/or emigration.

Benefiting from non-residence
If you are non-resident you are not liable to tax in this country on any income arising abroad. Income arising in this country is, however, subject to tax. If you are a UK citizen you are entitled to the personal allowances available, including age related married couple's allowance.

By concession from the Inland Revenue a person married to a person who has a full-time job abroad, and who accompanies their spouse, can benefit from the same non-resident status as their spouse. This is on the basis of the spouse's movements and employment, not their own.

If a person working abroad full time, and qualifying for the non-resident status, is not accompanied by their spouse, they can transfer any unused age related married couple's allowance to the spouse who is still in this country.

Capital Gains Tax and non-residence
If you are not resident in this country for the whole of a tax year, then any capital gain you make in that tax year is not liable to Capital Gains Tax. However, if you return to the UK before having been non-resident for five full tax years, then you will be liable to capital gains on any gains you made while non-resident, if you owned those assets at the time of your departure from this country.

TAX EFFICIENCY AUDIT

1. Are you able to affect the timing of your income? If so, could it benefit you?

2. Do you receive investment income in the way which is most tax efficient?

3. If you travel a lot in your business or work, have you arranged your affairs in the most tax efficient way?

4. Do you have any losses which could be used? Which is the most tax efficient way to use them?

5. Could you benefit from being non-resident? Have you weighed up the advantages and disadvantages?

5

Business Formats

CHOOSING THE RIGHT FORMAT FOR YOUR BUSINESS

Basically, the choices are as follows:

Limited company

This means that the limited company is the actual owner of the business. The ownership of the company depends on who holds the shares. It is possible for there to be just one shareholder, but this is not recommended. Shareholdings in the company are also a good way to pass on ownership of the company – say to the next generation of your family. The company has a separate legal existence from its shareholders, and is a method of protecting them – their liability is limited to the money they put into the business. A limited company must also have at least one director and one secretary. Again, it is recommended that there are always at least two directors.

Limited companies are liable to Corporation Tax. This is charged at rates between 0% and 32.75% (see details below).

Partnership

This consists of two or more people carrying on a business together. The terms of their partnership are governed by a partnership agreement, or if there is no partnership agreement, by the Partnership Act 1890.

Each partner is charged to income tax and class 4 National Insurance on their share of profits of the partnership for each tax year. You can be flexible about the way in which profits are shared between the partners, and this can produce savings on the total tax bill. It is often useful to be able to do this where a husband and wife are carrying out a business together.

Sole trader

This is the simplest form of carrying out a business. It simply consists of a person doing business on his or her own account. The person is charged to income tax and class 4 National Insurance on the business profits each year. A person can employ their husband or wife in their business, and pay them a salary. This will use up personal allowances, but the salary must actually be justified by the amount of work done. The salary must also be actually paid and recorded. It cannot be simply a book entry.

The decision whether to employ your spouse or be in partnership with him or her is one which depends on various circumstances – many of which are probably nothing to do with saving tax. However, all other things being equal, it is usually better and more flexible to be in partnership.

Question
Do I have complete freedom to choose in which format my business trades?

Answer
Yes, the choice is yours. There may be decision points in your business career when you have to think hard about it. For instance, you may be trading sole, and employing your wife or one of your children. The time may come when you have to think about taking them in to partnership. There may also be external pressures. In some industries, for example, people who can award you a contract may refuse to do so unless you are a limited company.

DECIDING TO GO LIMITED

Before deciding whether your business should be in the
format of a limited company or not, there are several
matters to consider.

Transferring an existing business

If you are thinking about making an existing business into a
limited company, you need to think about the actual transfer.
The limited company must buy the assets from you, the
existing trader. This could give rise to a Capital Gains Tax
liability. However, if the transfer is handled correctly, this can
be deferred. The solution is to issue shares in the new
company as the consideration for the assets of the business
bought. This effectively defers the Capital Gains Tax liability
until the shares are eventually sold – by that time you may
well qualify for retirement relief or taper relief. There are
three conditions which must be met:

1. The whole of the assets of the business must be
   transferred to the company.

2. The business must be transferred as a going concern.

3. The business must be transferred wholly or partly in
   exchange for shares issued by the company to the
   person(s) transferring the business.

However, when transferring a business to a limited
company, remember that Stamp Duty is payable on the
value of certain assets such as land, goodwill, debtors, etc.

How do you transfer a business to a company?
To transfer a business from yourself to a limited
company, you will probably need the help of a solicitor
and/or an accountant. A contract should be drawn up
encompassing the above points in the right form. A

limited company needs to be formed. There are many company registration agents who can register a company for you, either tailored to your specific requirements or an 'off the shelf' company which can be purchased. The date of registration of the company is not necessarily the same date as the start of trading of the business in its new format. That comes once the sale contract is agreed.

Tax tip
If you transfer a business from yourself to a limited company which you control, the Inland Revenue consider this as a transaction between connected persons. They will then seek to impose a market value on all trading stock which is transferred to the company. This will have the effect of making you taxable on the full selling price of trading stock before you have actually sold it. This could be especially costly where there is a large difference between the cost of the stock and the full selling price. A particular example of this would be a property developer who has land and developments in progress.

However, you can make an election for the trading stock to be transferred at the higher of the original cost or the amount paid by the company.

Starting a new business
If you start a new business as a limited company, you do not have the same problems as transferring a business. However, you do not have the same flexibility which is available to sole traders or partnerships. There are additional costs and compliance requirements attaching to limited companies. These include such things as stricter book keeping requirements, annual filing fees (and penalties for late delivery) with Companies House, possible audit requirements, stricter responsibilities for directors, stricter recording requirements for things such as meetings of

directors and shareholders, declaring dividends, issuing shares etc.

Weighing the benefits

The main taxation reason for trading as a limited company is that the Corporation Tax rate is:

- 0% on profits up to £10,000 per year

- 23.75% on profits between £10,001 and £50,000 per year

- 19% on profits between £50,001 and £300,000 per year

- 32.75% on profits between £300,001 and £1,500,000 per year

- 30% on profits above £1,500,000 per year.

This may seem a very favourable comparison to the higher income tax rate of 40% for all chargeable income in excess of £30,500 per year.

However, the corporation tax rate applies to profits of the company. The snag here is that the profits must remain in the company to bear the lower corporation tax rates. This is a good strategy if a large amount of the profits need to be ploughed back into the company. If, however, you want to benefit from the profits of the business personally, you have to draw the money out of the business. You can do this either by drawing a salary as a director, or by paying a dividend from the company on your shares. Either way, you will suffer tax at the higher income tax rates on the money you draw.

Drawing a salary

As a director drawing a salary, you will be liable not only for income tax, but also for class 1 National Insurance contributions. These would be greater in total than the combined tax and class 2 and 4 National Insurance liabilities for profits up to about £47,000 per year at present rates. In addition, the class 1 National Insurance contributions start to build up an earnings related supplement to the National Insurance pension when you retire. However, the class 1 liability falls on the company as well as the employee. The liability could be as much as 11% on the employee and 12.8% on the employer. Class 2 and class 4 contributions give you no extra benefits, but cost less.

How do you draw a salary from a company?
To draw a salary as a director you are on the same footing as any other employee. Therefore if you have not yet done so, you will need to contact your local tax office and register as an employer. They will then send you a pack of documentation to operate a PAYE system. This is the system by which the employer deducts tax and National Insurance from employees and then pays it over to the Inland Revenue once a month. You will then have to work out the deductions on the pay you are drawing as a director, and only draw the net amount.

Warning: There are some different rules for making National Insurance deductions for directors compared to ordinary employees.

Paying a dividend
Paying a dividend does of course avoid the class 1 National Insurance charge on both the company and the employee. The dividend carries a 10% tax credit, and there would be no further tax liability for lower rate and basic rate taxpayers. However, higher rate taxpayers have to pay the additional rate of 22.5%, but if you are not liable to tax, the tax credit is not repayable.

> **How do you draw dividends from a company?**
> To draw a dividend, you pay from the company to yourself the amount you wish to draw, but you must also account to the Inland Revenue for the tax credit. The company must also issue a divided voucher showing the net dividend paid and the tax credit. Do not forget to declare the dividend on your self-assessment tax return.

People running a business as a limited company often draw a mixture of salary and dividend.

Providing for a pension

A further advantage of running a business as a limited company is that the company can set up a company pension scheme for its directors (and other employees if required). The contribution limits are far more generous than for self-employed people, and the contributions of the company are tax deductible from its profits. If you are seriously considering the provision of a pension, a limited company could be a substantial advantage in planning your retirement.

> **How do you pay a pension in a company?**
> The company has to arrange a pension scheme, usually under the auspices of an insurance company which operates such schemes. Details such as who is allowed to join the scheme, what contributions are payable, what benefits are available and when, etc are included in the scheme rules. The scheme may be contributory, in which case the employees make some contribution which is matched by the employer, or non-contributory, in which case only the employer makes the contribution, and it is considered as a sort of benefit.

GOING INTO PARTNERSHIP

A partnership is legally defined as a body of persons carrying on business together with a view to profit. One of the most common types of partnership is between a husband and wife. The benefits for tax are such that this is an extremely popular way to carry on business. It confers flexibility of profit sharing arrangements which is one of the key advantages.

However, you must bear in mind that being in partnership creates certain duties and responsibilities. Also, the relationship between partners needs to be transparently open, because your partner can do things which will affect you – perhaps adversely. Husband and wife partnerships usually are not bound by a formal partnership agreement, but if you are entering on a partnership with somebody who is not your spouse it is extremely wise to draw up a partnership agreement.

If the Inland Revenue are doubtful about the validity of a partnership, they will apply tests to satisfy themselves. These tests include such things as:

- Is there a written partnership agreement?

- Is there any other evidence of a business partnership?

- What is the description of the business on the firm's stationery?

- Who has the authority to operate the business's bank account?

- Whose names appear on the VAT registration?

The presence of these tests indicates that there are tax advantages, and the Inland Revenue want to make sure that they are only taken advantage of by *bona fide* partnerships.

As indicated, one of the main benefits is that the profit

from the partnership can be divided out between the partners in a flexible way. Thus partners who have more allowances and reliefs for tax purposes could have more profit allocated to them so that they can make better use of their allowances, reliefs and lower rate tax bands. This all presumes that the method of sharing the profit is agreeable to all the partners.

This is why husband and wife partnerships are popular. In most cases the income from the business of a husband and wife partnership goes into the household 'purse'. How it is allocated between husband and wife does not matter except for tax purposes. A further allowance which produces savings is the class 4 National Insurance threshold.

Example:
Mr Jones is in business and he employs his wife at a salary of £4,000 a year. His profit after paying his wife's salary is £36,000 for 2003/2004. The tax liability is as follows:

		Husband	*Wife*
Profit		36,000	
Salary			4,000
Personal allowance		4,615	4,615
Taxable		31,385	Nil
Tax due:	10% on £1,960	196.00	
	22% on £28,540	6,278.80	
	40% on £885	354.00	
Total tax		6,828.80	
Class 4 National Insurance			
(30,940 − £4,615) × 8%		2,106.00	
£445 × 1%		4.45	
Total tax and class 4 liability		£8,939.25	

If Mr Jones took his wife into partnership, their profit figure would be £40,000. If the profits were divided equally, the position would be:

	Husband		*Wife*	
Profit	20,000		20,000	
Personal allowance	4,615		4,615	
Taxable		15,385		15,385
Tax due: 10% on £1,960	196.00		196.00	
22% on £13,425	2,953,50		2,953.50	
Total tax	3,149.50		3,149.50	
Class 4 National Insurance				
(£20,000 − £4,615) × 8%	1,230.80		1,230.80	
Total liability tax and Class 4	£4,380.30		£4,380.30	

The total tax and class 4 National Insurance bill is £8,760.60, compared to £8,939.25 if Mr Jones employed his wife.

Question
If it is so beneficial to take somebody into partnership, what is to stop me taking many more relatives, and other people, even the cat and the dog, into partnership?

Answer
There is nothing at all to stop you doing this (except for the cat and the dog). Many people running a family business bring their children into the partnership when the time is right. However, you must be sure you can work as equals with the people you take into partnership. Also, a partnership creates legal rights and obligations between the partners. One of the most important of these is the concept of joint and several liability. This means that if your partner owes any money, his creditors may pursue other members of the partnership for payment.

Dividing the profit
The profit does not have to be divided equally. If, in the above example, instead of dividing the profit equally, it were divided to the husband £33,425, and to the wife £6,575, the result would be as follows:

	Husband		Wife	
	Husband		*Wife*	
Profit	33,425		6,575	
Personal allowance	4,615		4,615	
Taxable		28,810		1,960
Tax due: 10% on £1,960	196.00		196.00	
22% on £26,850	5,907.00			
	6,103.00			
Class 4 National Insurance				
(£30,940 − £4,615) × 8%	2,106.00			
£2,485 × 1%	24.85			
£6,575 × £4,615) × 8%			156.80	
	£8,233.85		£352.80	

The total bill is now £8,586.65, a further saving of £173.95 compared to an equal sharing of the profit.

The key to deciding how to divide profits is to use the allowances and lower rate tax bands as far as possible. In some cases, as in the above example, it means trading off a smaller charge against a larger one. In the above example, if the wife had been allocated £4,615 of the profit, and the husband £35,385, she would have saved the 8% class 4 charge. However, this would have been at the expense of the husband paying 40% tax on most of the extra.

How do you divide profits in a partnership?
The division of profits should be shown on the face of your partnership accounts. If each partner has a separate capital account, their share of the profit should be added to their capital account. This division of profits should be the same as that on the partnership self-assessment tax return, boxes 11 to 29 on pages 6 and 7 of the partnership tax return (see Figures 19 and 20).

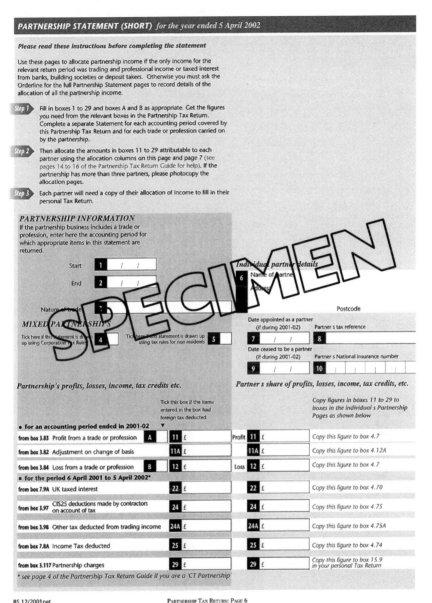

PARTNERSHIP STATEMENT (SHORT) *for the year ended 5 April 2002*

Please read these instructions before completing the statement

Use these pages to allocate partnership income if the only income for the relevant return period was trading and professional income or taxed interest from banks, building societies or deposit takers. Otherwise you must ask the Orderline for the full Partnership Statement pages to record details of the allocation of all the partnership income.

Step 1 Fill in boxes 1 to 29 and boxes A and B as appropriate. Get the figures you need from the relevant boxes in the Partnership Tax Return. Complete a separate Statement for each accounting period covered by this Partnership Tax Return and for each trade or profession carried on by the partnership.

Step 2 Then allocate the amounts in boxes 11 to 29 attributable to each partner using the allocation columns on this page and page 7 (see pages 14 to 16 of the Partnership Tax Return Guide for help). If the partnership has more than three partners, please photocopy the allocation pages.

Step 3 Each partner will need a copy of their allocation of income to fill in their personal Tax Return.

PARTNERSHIP INFORMATION

If the partnership business includes a trade or profession, enter here the accounting period for which appropriate items in this statement are returned.

Start **1** / /

End **2** / /

Nature of trade **3**

MIXED PARTNERSHIPS

Tick here if this statement is drawn up using Corporation Tax Rules **4**

Tick here if this statement is drawn up using tax rules for non residents **5**

Individual partner details

6 Name of partner

Address

Postcode

Date appointed as a partner (if during 2001-02) **7** / /

Partner's tax reference **8**

Date ceased to be a partner (if during 2001-02) **9** / /

Partner's National Insurance number **10**

Partnership's profits, losses, income, tax credits etc.

Partner's share of profits, losses, income, tax credits, etc.

Tick this box if the items entered in the box had foreign tax deducted ▼

Copy figures in boxes 11 to 29 to boxes in the individual's Partnership Pages as shown below

● for an accounting period ended in 2001-02

from box 3.83 Profit from a trade or profession **A**	**11** £	Profit **11** £	Copy this figure to box 4.7
from box 3.82 Adjustment on change of basis	**11A** £	**11A** £	Copy this figure to box 4.12A
from box 3.84 Loss from a trade or profession **B**	**12** £	Loss **12** £	Copy this figure to box 4.7

● for the period 6 April 2001 to 5 April 2002*

from box 7.9A UK taxed interest	**22** £	**22** £	Copy this figure to box 4.70
from box 3.97 CIS25 deductions made by contractors on account of tax	**24** £	**24** £	Copy this figure to box 4.75
from box 3.98 Other tax deducted from trading income	**24A** £	**24A** £	Copy this figure to box 4.75A
from box 7.8A Income Tax deducted	**25** £	**25** £	Copy this figure to box 4.74
from box 3.117 Partnership charges	**29** £	**29** £	Copy this figure to box 15.9 in your personal Tax Return

* see page 4 of the Partnership Tax Return Guide if you are a 'CT Partnership'

Fig. 19. Page 6 of partnership self-assessment tax return.

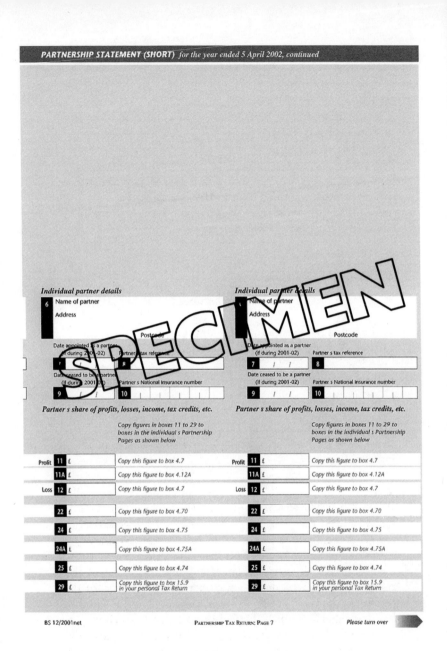

Fig. 20. Page 7 of partnership self-assessment tax return.

Question
Can the Inspector of Taxes challenge the division of profits if it seems too artificial?

Answer
No. As long as there is nothing in a partnership agreement which forbids it, and as long as the figures in the partnership accounts agree with the tax figures, you may allocate the profits in whatever way you wish.

BUYING A BUSINESS

It is important to differentiate between:

- buying a business as a going concern
- buying the assets of a business
- and buying the shares in a company which is carrying on a business.

There are significant differences in the tax treatment of these three methods. For example, the VAT treatment is quite different.

VAT
If you buy a business as a going concern there is no VAT to pay on the transaction. If you buy assets of a business, there is VAT to be charged by the seller. If you buy the shares in a company there is no VAT on the transaction. There is also a continuing VAT implication. If you buy the shares of the company you are becoming an owner, or part owner, of the business. The company's VAT registration is not affected, and you inherit any possible liabilities to VAT which may emerge at a later date. Also, the company may be part of a VAT group of companies, and all members of a VAT group

are liable for each others' VAT liabilities. If another member of the group became insolvent, the Customs and Excise could come back on other members of the group to pay the liability of the insolvent member.

Even when buying a business as a going concern, you need to be vigilant. In this transaction you are asked by the Customs and Excise whether you want to take over the registration of the existing business. If you say yes to this, once again you inherit the existing business's VAT liabilities.

Stamp Duty

The Stamp Duty treatment is also different. If you buy shares in the company there is Stamp Duty to pay at ½% on the value of the shares. If you buy the business as a going concern, or the assets of the business, Stamp Duty is payable at a sliding scale between 0% and 4% depending on the value. You therefore need to work out the Stamp Duty in each case.

Corporation Tax and Income Tax

If you buy the shares in a company, and it continues to carry on the same trade, then any losses which may have accumulated are available to carry forward against future profits. Any assets on which capital allowances have been claimed will simply continue to be carried forward at their written down value.

If you buy the business as a going concern, or the assets of a business, you are treated as starting a new business for income tax purposes. The price which you paid for the assets will be their cost for the purposes of capital allowances. It does not matter what value they had been written down to by the predecessor, you start off at the price you paid.

SELLING A BUSINESS

Selling a business presents the same sort of considerations as buying a business, but from the other side of the fence. However, there are certain other considerations.

Selling a company

If the business you are selling is a limited company, then you need to consider the way in which you sell it. A buyer may merely want to buy the business as a going concern, or the assets of the business, without buying the shares which give him ownership of the company. However, from your point of view this presents a difficult problem.

If a company sells assets or the business as a going concern, then the company is liable to Capital Gains Tax on the transaction. Further, when you want to get your money out of the company, there is a further Capital Gains or Corporation Tax charge.

By far the best and simplest means of selling a business owned by a company is to sell the shares of the company. This way, there is only one Capital Gains Tax charge.

How do you sell a business?
The way in which you sell a limited company will depend largely on your negotiating skills, and the expertise of your solicitor in drawing up the sale document in the right form. Make sure there are no loose ends.

TAX EFFICIENCY AUDIT

1. Have you decided on your business format by a conscious decision, or by default?

2. Have you set out the benefits and disadvantages to you of going limited?

3. Are you employing any members of your family in your business? If so, could you take them into partnership?

4. Are you contemplating buying or selling a business? If so, have you sought advice about the timing implications and the VAT aspect?

5. If you are thinking about going into partnership with other people, have you considered the aspects apart from tax which might affect your decision?

6

Corporation Tax

As we saw in Chapter 2 companies must complete self-assessment Corporation Tax returns in the same way as individuals. However, the way in which Corporation Tax works, and the tax rates, are quite different.

TAX RATES

Corporation Tax is the tax which limited companies pay. It is charged at different rates from Income Tax. This sometimes gives rise to opportunities for tax planning. If the Corporation Tax rate is different from the Income Tax rate, it makes sense to try to get your income taxed at the lowest rate available. The rates of Corporation Tax for 2002/2003 are:

Profits	Rate of tax
up to £10,000	0%
£10,001 to £50,000	23.75%
£50,001 to £300,000	19%
£300,001 to £1,500,000	32.75%
over £1,500,000	30%

The technical explanation of the rates between £10,001 and £50,000, and between £300,001 and £1,500,000, is rather more complicated than shown above. However, the effect is that the tax rate on those bands of profits is higher than the next band of profits.

Special cases

There is an exception to the general allocation of tax rates. This applies to 'close investment-holding companies'. A close company is one which is controlled by five or fewer people. An investment-holding company is one which does not trade but gets its income from investments. All income of close investment-holding companies is taxed at 30%.

There is also a special rate of tax of 25% on 'loans to participators' made by a 'close company'. 'Participators' are shareholders, and certain types of loan creditors. 'Close companies', as we have seen, are those controlled by five or fewer individuals.

If a close company makes a loan to a participator, there is a Corporation Tax charge of 25% on that amount. The tax is payable nine months after the end of the accounting period in which the loan is made. However, if the loan is repaid within nine months after the end of the accounting period during which it was made, then the tax does not become payable. If the loan is repaid by the participator after the tax is paid, the tax can be reclaimed nine months after the end of the accounting period in which the loan is repaid.

FINANCIAL YEARS AND ACCOUNTING PERIODS

Corporation Tax is calculated on financial years ended on 31 March, unlike Income Tax when 5 April is the year end.

The profits are calculated on the company's accounting period, and that accounting period is allocated over the financial years into which it falls. This again is different from Income Tax, when the tax rate is determined by the date on which the business's year ends.

Example

A company's year ends on 30 September. For the year ended 30 September 2003, the profits are divided between the year ended 31 March 2003, and 31 March 2004. Thus, six months of the profit are taxed in the 2002/2003 financial year, and the other six months of the profit are taxed in the 2003/2004 financial year. In this case there is no difference between the rates of tax in those two financial years. However, if the example had been two years earlier, there would have been a difference, because the rates of tax changed from 1 April 2001.

The profits are allocated between the two years purely on a time basis. It could be that the profits were earned disproportionately in the two periods, but the total profits for the year are still time-apportioned for these purposes.

Corporation Tax is always charged for periods which cannot exceed 12 months. It sometimes happens that a company has an accounting period of more or less than 12 months.

- If the accounting period is less than 12 months, the same period is used for Corporation Tax.

- If the accounting period is more than 12 months, the Corporation Tax charge is based on a 12-month period (always the first 12 months of the accounting period), and the remaining period is charged separately.

Example
A company's accounting period is from 1 January 2003 to 31 March 2004. The Corporation Tax charge is divided into the 12 months ended 31 December 2003, and the three months ended 31 March 2004.

Company law prohibits regular and frequent changes of accounting date, so this cannot happen in successive years.

COMPANY RESIDENCE

UK Corporation Tax is charged on:

- UK resident companies, and

- non-resident companies carrying on a trade in the UK through a branch or agency (but only on the income and capital gains arising through that UK activity).

  The definition of a UK resident company is:

- any company incorporated in the UK since 15 March 1988

- any company of which the control and management is exercised in the UK.

UK resident companies are taxed on all their income and capital gains, whether they arose in the UK or abroad. However, where the company has paid foreign tax on its overseas income or capital gains, they may be granted double taxation relief. If the foreign tax exceeds the UK tax, that foreign tax constitutes an 'unrelieved foreign tax credit'. This may be carried back up to three years, and carried forward indefinitely.

Controlled foreign companies

Special rules apply where:

- a UK company controls a foreign company, and

- the foreign company is in a 'low tax' jurisdiction – ie if the overseas tax is less than 75% of the equivalent UK tax.

The special rules are that, where the UK company controls at least 10% of the foreign company, a proportion of the overseas income of the foreign company is apportioned to it and charged to UK Corporation Tax. However, if the foreign company distributes at least 90% of its profits to its shareholders, this charge does not apply.

ASSOCIATED COMPANIES

The concept of associated companies can affect the structure of groups of companies or different companies under common control. The reason for this is that where two or more companies are 'associated' with each other, the band limits shown above are divided between the number of associated companies.

Example
If there are four associated companies, the bands of Corporation Tax rates for each company are as follows:

Profits	Rate of tax
up to £2,500	0%
£2,501 to £12,500	23.75%
£12,501 to £75,000	19%
£75,001 to £375,000	32.75%
over £375,000	30%

It is therefore important to understand what 'associated companies' are. The basic definition is simple – associated companies are those companies under common control or where one company controls the other. This gives rise to a number of other points:

- The formal structure of companies is not the final test of 'control'. Thus, if two companies are in a relationship of parent and subsidiary, that is usually an indication of control of the subsidiary by the parent company. However, there does not have to be this formal structural relationship. Control is looked at according to the commercial reality.

- Associated companies are counted for these purposes even if the association was for part of the accounting period only.

119

- Two or more companies associated to the 'base' company can be counted even if they were associated at different parts of the accounting period, and they will all count fully towards the number of associated companies.

However, there are circumstances under which associated companies are disregarded. These are:

- If a company has not carried out any trade or business during the accounting period, or the part of the period during which it was associated.

- If a non-trading holding company (ie a company which merely holds shares in another company or companies)
  - has no assets other than the shares in its subsidiaries, or
  - has no income or gains other than dividends from these shares, and these dividends are distributed in full to its shareholders, or
  - has no entitlement to a Corporation Tax deduction for charges or management expenses.

GROUPS OF COMPANIES

A group of companies exists where there is a structure of parent and subsidiary companies, and where:

- one company owns at least 75% of the other company, or
- a third company owns at least 75% of each company.

The rules for taxing groups of companies exist separately from the rules about associated companies. The main features of group companies' taxation are as follows:

Group relief
Trading losses and other eligible reliefs in one company can

be set against profits of any other company in the same group. If there is a non-resident company in the group, it may take advantage of this group relief if it is carrying on a trade in the UK through a branch.

Rollover relief
A capital gain from the sale of a qualifying asset can be 'rolled over' against the purchase of another qualifying asset by any other company of the same group. This also extends to non-resident companies trading in the UK through a branch, if the new asset is purchased for the UK branch. This thereby defers the gain in the group as a whole.

Transfers of assets
Assets can be transferred to other companies in the group on a no gain/no loss basis. It is also possible to make a special election that the disposal of an asset for Capital Gains Tax purposes should be treated as if it had been disposed of by any other company in the group.

Transfer of losses carried forward
Losses can be transferred from any company in a group to any other, when the trade of the transferring company is transferred.

CAPITAL GAINS

Unlike individuals, companies do not pay a separate Capital Gains Tax. Instead, any capital gains are added to the company's income to arrive at the amount chargeable to Corporation Tax. The calculation of capital gains is made in the same way as the calculation for individuals *except*:

• There is no annual capital gains exemption for companies.

- Taper relief is not available to companies.

- Indexation relief continues to be available to companies. (It was abolished in 1998 for individuals.)

- Capital losses cannot normally be offset against profits or other income. They may only be carried forward against future capital gains.

These differences in treatment mean that sometimes it is more beneficial to have a capital gain taxed on a company, and sometimes more beneficial to have it taxed as an individual. The variables can affect the calculations in different ways.

TAX EFFICIENCY AUDIT

1. Are your accounting systems adequate, *and up to date,* to enable you to complete the Corporation Tax return in time?

2. Are you able to stay out of the 'higher' rates of tax of 23.75% and 32.75%?

3. If your business is complex, could it be structured in a way to enable it to benefit from the group reliefs and advantages?

7

Value Added Tax

VAT – A QUICK GUIDE

Value Added Tax was conceived as a simple tax. A flat rate of tax was to be added on to all 'outputs' of businesses, and paid over to the Commissioners of Customs and Excise. Part of its complexity today is due to the fact that it is administered by the Customs and Excise, rather than by the Inland Revenue. Getting it wrong can be very costly, and there are swingeing penalties for getting it wrong.

The principle of VAT is that a business adds output tax to its sales. If it sells to another VAT registered business, that business may claim relief for tax it has paid on its purchases and expenses (its **input tax**) against its own **output tax**.

Another part of the complexity arises from the way in which VAT is added to outputs of a supplier, then claimed back by the purchaser. The chain goes right along the line from the initial supplier of raw materials to the final consumer, who is not able to claim back the tax. There are also different rates of tax for different items, and a distinction between zero-rated items and exempt items.

AVOIDING VAT PITFALLS

The main danger areas in VAT are:

- registration and deregistration
- claiming input tax
- paying output tax.

REGISTERING AND DEREGISTERING

Knowing when to register for VAT

A business has to register for VAT if its turnover is above a certain limit. This limit changes from year to year, and at the time of writing is £56,000 per year. The limit counts for any 12 consecutive months.

If you start in business you should keep a record of your business turnover, month by month. When you reach 12 months, you need only keep a record for these purposes of the last 12 months' figures.

Example

	Turnover	Cumulative turnover 12 months
Month 1	1,000	1,000
Month 2	2,000	3,000
Month 3	4,000	7,000
Month 4	5,000	12,000
Month 5	6,000	18,000
Month 6	6,000	24,000
Month 7	6,000	30,000
Month 8	6,000	36,000
Month 9	6,000	42,000
Month 10	3,000	45,000
Month 11	4,000	49,000
Month 12	2,500	51,500
Month 13	6,000	56,500

You will see that the registration point of £56,000 for any 12 consecutive months has not been reached until the thirteenth month. In keeping a running total, once you get past 12 months the latest month's figure is added, but the earliest one is then dropped off the total.

Once the registration point has been reached you have 30 days to notify the Customs and Excise of your liability to register. They will then register you from the following month. You are also liable to register if there are reasonable grounds for believing that your turnover will exceed the registration limit in the next 30 days.

Registering voluntarily

Tax tip

You have the option to register for VAT voluntarily even if your turnover does not reach the registration limit. Why would you want to do this?

The most obvious circumstance in which it might be beneficial to register voluntarily is when you have zero-rated outputs, in which case you do not have to add VAT to your sales. However, because you are registered you may claim back the input tax on the expenses you incur. This could represent a considerable saving.

If your turnover consists of rated goods or services, it is obvious that having to add VAT to your sales will increase the prices you have to charge your customers. This could make you less competitive, and destroy any advantage of being able to claim back the input tax. However, it all depends on whether your customers are mainly the general public or other registered traders.

If your customers are mainly the general public, then having to add VAT to your sales is a disadvantage. However, if your customers are mainly other registered businesses, then it does not matter whether you add VAT to your sales or not. If you do add it, your customers can claim it back as their input tax.

How do you register for VAT?
You register by writing to your local Customs and Excise office. (You can find their telephone and address in the telephone directory.) They will send you a registration form (see Figure 21) to complete.

Part 1   About the business

Name

1 **Sole proprietors** – please give your full name.

Partnerships – please give your trading name, or if you do not have one please give the names of all partners. You must also complete and return form VAT 2 (available from the National Advice Service or our website).

Corporate or unincorporated bodies – please give the name of the company, club, association, etc.

2 **Do you have a trading name?** (Please tick)   ☐ Yes   ☐ No

Please give the trading name of the business.

Status

3 **What is the structure/legal status of the business?** (Please tick)

☐ Sole proprietor   ☐ Partnership (Please complete form VAT 2)

☐ Corporate body (e.g. limited company)

Please give incorporation details: Certificate no.

Date of incorporation

Country of incorporation

☐ Unincorporated body (e.g. club or association)

Please specify

Business address

4 **Please give the address of your principal place of business. This is where you carry out most of the day-to-day running of the business.** e.g. where you receive and deal with orders.

Postcode

Business phone

Fax number

Mobile phone

E-mail address

Internet address

Fig. 21. VAT registration form (page one of seven).

You then have to comply with all the book keeping requirements, and you will have to complete a VAT return regularly.

Knowing when to deregister

You may have been registered for VAT, but would be better off if you did not have to be registered and add VAT to your sales. If the volume of your business has decreased, you can deregister from VAT. The turnover must be at or below the deregistration limit which, at the time of writing, is £54,000 in any consecutive 12-month period.

Tax tip

If your business turnover is only marginally over the deregistration limit, you could actually be better off by decreasing your business turnover, so that you can deregister. The saving on VAT could then more than offset the loss in turnover. However, you do need to be sure that there is no prospect of your turnover increasing substantially, at least in the near future.

If you deregister, however, you must pay over VAT on business assets which you had at the date of deregistration, and on which you had originally claimed VAT input tax. The value on which to work out the VAT for these purposes is the value of identical or similar goods of the same age and condition. However, if the VAT on these business assets does not exceed £250, you may ignore it for these purposes.

How do you deregister from VAT?
You deregister from VAT by writing to your Customs and Excise office to tell them that you wish to do so. You will be sent a final VAT return to complete up to the date of deregistration.

Business splitting

You may think it is possible to get round the need to register for VAT by splitting a business down into two or more sections, each of which is below the registration limit. Thus, if a shop has a turnover of £60,000 per year, is it possible to say that there are two businesses, one consisting of tobacco and cigarette sales, the other of confectionery and newspaper sales, each with a turnover below £56,000 per year? The answer is no. The Customs and Excise have anti-avoidance powers to stop this. In consequence, businesses must be genuinely separate to be 'disaggregated'.

This means that, amongst other things, the following characteristics must be there:

- Separate ownership – either the husband must own one business and the wife the other, or one spouse owns one business and a partnership or limited company owns the other.

- Separate equipment and premises. Normally, separate businesses must operate from separate premises and use separate equipment.

- Records must be kept separately for each business.

- Invoices to and from each business must be in the name of that business.

- Wages paid to employees must be paid separately by each business.

- For Income Tax purposes each business must be separate.

CLAIMING INPUT TAX

The basic principle of claiming input tax is that you may claim for items that can be attributed, either directly or indirectly, to taxable supplies you make.

Zero-rated or exempt? The vital difference

The distinction between zero-rated and exempt items is crucial. If your output consists of zero-rated items, you are allowed to offset input tax against the output tax on your sales. However, if your output consists of exempt items, you may not deduct the input tax. There are special rules and calculations for a business which has partial exemption – ie a mix of rated and exempt items.

Distinguishing business and private items

You may only claim back input tax on business items. This may seem an obvious point, but a surprisingly large number of people try to claim back input tax on private items.

Getting the right documentation

In order to claim input tax you must have a valid tax invoice from the supplier. To be valid it must:

- have the supplier's VAT number on it
- have the supplier's name and address
- be addressed to you
- be dated
- show the detail of the goods or services supplied
- show the total amount before tax
- show the tax rate
- show the amount of tax
- show the total amount including tax.

However, a less detailed tax invoice is allowed for goods sold if the total amount is less than £100. This less detailed tax invoice need only show:

- the supplier's name and address, and VAT registration number
- the date
- the description of the goods

- the total amount including tax
- the tax rate.

VAT input tax is not claimable on delivery notes, or pro-forma invoices, or if the invoice states 'this is not a tax invoice'.

Specific exclusions

Certain items are specifically excluded for the purpose of claiming input tax. Here are some of the most important:

Motor cars

Input tax cannot be claimed on the cost of a motor car if there is any private use of it. This rule is interpreted very strictly by Customs and Excise. In practice it is very rare to get a claim for input tax on a motor car allowed. The circumstances have to be such that there is no possibility of private use. Note however the following:

- VAT on lease rentals of cars and contract hire of cars may be claimed, but only up to a maximum of 50%.

- VAT on vans, lorries, motor cycles, etc can be claimed as long as all the normal conditions are met.

Entertaining

VAT on the cost of entertaining customers cannot be claimed as input tax. This applies whether the customer is from this country or overseas. Entertaining is interpreted widely, and covers almost any type of hospitality.

However, entertaining staff is allowable. If there is an occasion when staff and guests or customers are also present, the cost should be apportioned. Only the input tax attributable to the staff may be claimed.

Director's accommodation
VAT incurred on supplying any domestic accommodation
for a director of a company is not claimable. However, hotel
costs for directors (and employees) is claimable. Once again,
if there is accommodation for a mixture of directors, staff,
and guests or customers, the amount must be apportioned,
and only the costs for directors and staff may be claimed.

Non-payment
If you do not pay your supplier, for whatever reason, then
you may not reclaim the tax. The supplier, if he writes off
your debt, will inform the Customs and Excise of your name
and address.

PAYING OUTPUT TAX

It is important to charge the correct rate of tax on your
supplies. The principle is that you, as a taxable person, must
account for VAT at the right rate on taxable supplies you
make. Difficulties sometimes arise in deciding what is the
correct rate of tax, and what constitutes a taxable supply.

Food products – what is zero-rated?
In deciding what is zero-rated and what is standard-rated,
be especially aware of the regulations concerning food.
    The general rule is that food products are zero-rated. This
includes:

- food for human consumption
- animal feeding stuffs
- seeds or other propagation of plants coming within the
  above two categories
- live animals generally used as food for human
  consumption.

However, there are several important exceptions. Perhaps the most obvious is catering. Food supplied in the course of catering is standard-rated. But what is catering? It is described as any supply of food or drink for consumption on the premises where it is sold. However, the sale of takeaway foods (ie hot food sold for consumption off the premises) is also within this category for standard-rating.

But where do you draw the line between, say, a takeaway curry and a loaf of bread that is sold at a bakery while it is still hot? There are detailed guidelines, and you have to work out for yourself what category your sales come under. The penalty for getting it wrong could be great.

Other important food exceptions which are standard-rated are:

- Confectionery and chocolate products. There is a fairly detailed distinction between zero-rated and standard-rated items. For instance, chocolate-covered biscuits are standard-rated, but chocolate spread is zero-rated. Cakes are zero-rated, but compressed fruit and nut bars are standard-rated. Toffee as a confectionery is standard-rated, but toffee apples are zero-rated. You begin to see how complex these matters can be.

- Ice cream and similar frozen products.

- Alcoholic drinks.

- Non-alcoholic beverages such as fruit juices, syrups, concentrates etc.

(However, tea, coffee, cocoa, and milk are the most important items still zero-rated.)

- Crisps and salted or roasted nuts.

- Home brewing materials.

Fuel scale charges

If you claim VAT input tax relief on fuel for cars, and you have any private use during the VAT period, then you must add a 'scale charge' to your VAT output tax which you pay over to Customs and Excise. This represents a taxable supply.

This scale charge is a fixed amount, dependent on the size of the engine of the car, as shown in the following table. However, it is fixed irrespective of the amount of private usage you have of the car. No matter whether you use the car 90% for private use or 5%, the scale charge is the same.

Table of scale charges for the year ended 5 April 2004:

	12 months charge	VAT due	3 months charge	VAT due	1 months charge	VAT due
Diesel engine cars						
up to 2,000cc	£900	£134.04	£225	£33.51	£75	£11.17
over 2,000cc	£1,135	£169.04	£283	£42.14	£94	£14.00
Petrol engine cars						
up to 1,400cc	£950	£141.48	£237	£35.29	£79	£11.76
1401cc – 2,000cc	£1,200	£178.72	£300	£44.68	£100	£14.89
over 2,000cc	£1,770	£263.61	£442	£65.82	£147	£21.89

Tax tip

If the total amount spent on fuel for cars is below the amount of the 'charge' figure shown in the above table, you are better off not claiming the input tax on the fuel. Otherwise, the scale charge would exceed the input tax you claim.

Supplies of goods for private purposes

If you are registered for VAT, you must pay output tax on any supplies for which you have recovered input tax, when you take those goods out of the business for private use. If, for example, you own a clothing shop, and take clothes for your own or your family's use, you must account for output tax. The amount at which you must calculate the tax is on the cost to the business, not the normal selling price.

Non-business use of assets
If a business asset is made available without charge, for a non-business use, then output tax must be accounted for on the full cost to the business of making the asset available.

Deemed supply on deregistration
Where a business deregisters, there is a 'deemed' supply of the goods and assets held at the time of deregistration. If VAT input tax had previously been claimed then it must be paid over as output tax (calculated on the value to the business of the goods in their present state at deregistration). However, if the VAT on the deemed supply does not exceed £250, it may be disregarded.

Barter and exchange
If a transaction does not involve a money exchange, it should nevertheless be calculated for the purpose of paying over output tax. This applies to goods or services. Therefore, if there is any barter or exchange of goods or services, the normal commercial values must be taken into account, for input tax and output tax.

Annual accounting scheme
Businesses with a turnover up to £600,000 per year may join the annual accounting scheme, which allows them to make one VAT return per year. Normally, the business must have been registered at least one year before joining this scheme, but if the taxable turnover is up to £150,000, that business may join the scheme immediately.

A provisional VAT liability is agreed with Customs and Excise. Then, if the turnover is above £150,000, the provisional figure is divided by ten. Nine monthly payments of that tenth are made by direct debit, starting four months after the beginning of their financial year. The balancing payment must then be made, together with the annual VAT return, within two months after the end of the financial year.

If the turnover is up to £150,000, the provisional figure is divided by four, and instead of nine monthly payments, the business makes three quarterly payments of the calculated 25% of the provisional figure.

If the business's turnover reaches £750,000, it must withdraw from the scheme.

Flat rate scheme

Businesses with taxable VAT-exclusive turnover of up to £150,000 and total VAT-exclusive turnover of up to £187,5000 may join the flat rate scheme.

Under this scheme, instead of calculating input tax and output tax, the business calculates one flat rate of VAT on its turnover. The actual flat rate is given according to the business's trade sector. This applies to all the turnover, including reduced rate, zero rate, and exempt supplies. Where there are normally different rates of tax which would apply, this is taken into account by the flat rate for that particular sector.

The business issues invoices to other VAT registered customers in the same way as previously, showing the normal VAT rate. However,instead of making separate calculations of input and output tax, the calculation is at just one figure, and that is what is paid over to Customs and Excise. However, the business may recover input tax on capital goods acquired with a value of more than £2,000. If those goods are subsequently sold, the applicable output VAT must be accounted for separately from the flat rate VAT.

TAX EFFICIENCY AUDIT

1. If you are not registered for VAT, do you have a system to enable you to monitor your turnover?

2. Could you benefit from voluntary registration?

3. If you are registered, and your turnover is low, could you benefit from deregistering?

4. Do you ensure that you always get a valid tax invoice to reclaim the input tax?

5. Do you keep the rates for fuel scale charges updated? Could you benefit by not reclaiming the input tax on motor fuel?

6. Could you benefit from joining the annual accounting scheme or the flat rate scheme?

8

Capital Gains Tax

USING YOUR ANNUAL ALLOWANCE

As with Income Tax, everybody has a personal allowance
for Capital Gains Tax purposes. For the 2003/2004 tax year
the allowance is £7,900 per person. There is also a degree of
'allowance' in the way in which Capital Gains Tax is
charged.

How Capital Gains Tax is charged

Capital Gains Tax is charged by adding the amount of the
gain to your other income charged to Income Tax, and
charging tax at the top marginal savings rate. This could
result in a charge at two or even three different rates.

Example
Your income for the 2003/2004 tax year is £25,000, and you
have capital gains of £20,000 for the same year. The tax is
worked out as follows:

Income	25,000	
Personal allowance	4,615	
Taxable		20,385
Income tax due:		
10% on £1,960		196.00
22% on £18,425		4,053.30
Total income tax due		4,249.50
Capital Gains	20,000	
Annual exemption	7,900	
Taxable	£12,100	

Capital Gains Tax due:

20% on £10,115	2023.00
40% on £1,985	794.00
Total Capital Gains Tax	£2,817.00

You will therefore be able to pay less Capital Gains Tax if you can use up your personal allowance, or if you can keep your chargeable tax to the next lowest band. In the above example, if you had been able to reduce your gain chargeable to tax by £1,985, you would have avoided paying tax at the 40% rate.

Tax tip
Remember also that a husband and wife each have a personal allowance and all the reduced rate tax bands.

Using losses
So how can you keep your capital gains down to the limits to save tax? One important tool is to use the losses which may be available. All transactions producing capital gains or losses within the same tax year are merged together for tax purposes.

Tax tip
If you have gains which are over the threshold limit, consider whether you may be able to do any other transactions which would produce a loss for capital gains purposes.

Example
You have various stocks and shares, and you have actively traded several of them during the tax year. So far you have produced gains of £8,500. If you can produce losses of £600 you could reduce your gains to the threshold limit and avoid any tax liability.

Tax tip

It may be possible to establish a loss without actually disposing of any assets. If you have assets which have decreased in value, and are now of negligible value, you can make a claim to 'crystallise' the loss. In practice this applies most frequently to shares in companies which are no longer of any value. For instance, some years ago the shares in Maxwell Communications became of no value following the death of Robert Maxwell. The Inland Revenue recognises shares as being of negligible value when their value has decreased to 5% or less of their nominal value. Therefore, if £1 shares are worth 5p or less, they are recognised for this purpose.

The advantage of this provision is that you do not have to declare them as being of negligible value straight away. You may wait until you can benefit from it, and then make the claim for the loss.

How do you use losses?

Losses are set off against gains automatically. No special claim is needed. Enter all your transactions on pages 2 and 3 of the capital gains pages of your self-assessment tax return (see Figures 22 and 23). The gains are totalled and the losses are totalled separately. The gains are then entered in box 8.7 of page 8 of the capital gains pages (see Figure 24). The losses are entered in box 8.10.

Keeping your gains within the limits

Another way of utilising the threshold limit is to ensure that your gains come up to the limit.

Example

You have made gains so far in the tax year of £4,000. If you can make further gains of up to £3,900 you will still not be liable to tax, because you are still within your limit.

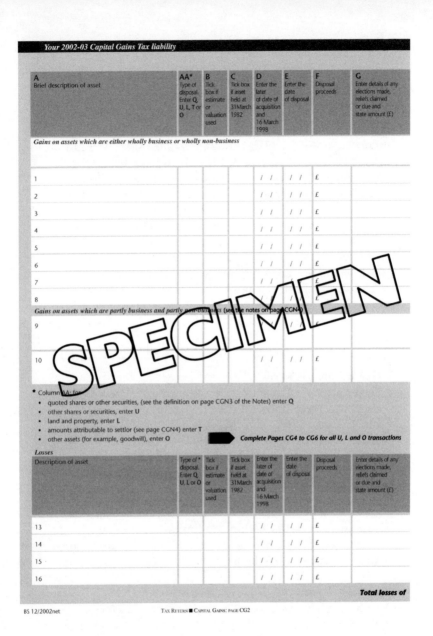

Fig. 22. Page 2 of capital gains pages of self-assessment tax return.

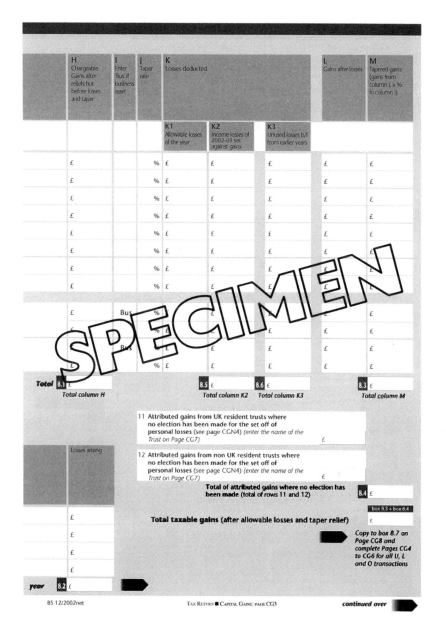

H Chargeable Gains after reliefs but before losses and taper	I Enter 'Bus' if business asset	J Taper rate	K Losses deducted			L Gains after losses	M Tapered gains (gains from column L x % in column J)
			K1 Allowable losses of the year	K2 Income losses of 2002-03 set against gains	K3 Unused losses b/f from earlier years		
£		%	£	£	£	£	£
£		%	£	£	£	£	£
£		%	£	£	£	£	£
£		%	£	£	£	£	£
£		%	£	£	£	£	£
£		%	£	£	£	£	£
£		%	£	£	£	£	£
£	Bus	%	£	£	£	£	£
£		%	£	£	£	£	£
£	Bus	%	£	£	£	£	£
£		%	£	£	£	£	£

Total | 8.1 £
Total column H

8.5 £
Total column K2 | 8.6 £
Total column K3

8.3 £
Total column M

11 Attributed gains from UK resident trusts where no election has been made for the set off of personal losses (see page CGN4) *(enter the name of the Trust on Page CG7)* £

12 Attributed gains from non UK resident trusts where no election has been made for the set off of personal losses (see page CGN4) *(enter the name of the Trust on Page CG7)* £

Total of attributed gains where no election has been made (total of rows 11 and 12) 8.4 £

box 8.3 + box 8.4

Total taxable gains (after allowable losses and taper relief) £

Copy to box 8.7 on Page CG8 and complete Pages CG4 to CG6 for all U, L and O transactions

Losses arising

£

£

£

£

year | 8.2 £

Fig. 23. Page 3 of capital gains pages of self-assessment tax return.7

Once you have completed Page CG1, or Pages CG2 to CG6, fill in this Page.

Have you 'ticked' any row in Column B, 'Tick box if estimate or valuation used' on Pages CG1 or CG2 or in Column C on Page CG2 'Tick box if asset held at 31 March 1982'? **NO** **YES**

Have you given details in Column G on Pages CG2 and CG3 of any Capital Gains reliefs claimed or due? **NO** **YES**

Are you claiming, and/or using, any 'clogged' losses (see Notes, page CGN10)? **NO** **YES**

Enter the number of transactions from Page CG1 or column AA on Page CG2 for:

- transactions in quoted shares or other securities **box Q**
- transactions in other shares or securities **box U**
- transactions in land and property **box L**
- other transactions **box O**

Total taxable gains (from Page CG1 or Page CG3) **8.7** £

Your taxable gains *minus* the annual exempt amount of £7,500 (leave blank if '0' or negative) — box 8.7 *minus* £7,500 **8.8** £

Additional liability in respect of non-resident or dual resident trusts (see Notes, page CGN6) **8.9** £

Capital losses

(If your loss arose on a transaction with a connected person, see Notes page CGN13, you can only set that loss against gains you make on disposals to that same connected person.)

■ **This year's losses**

- Total (from box 8.2 on Page CG3 or box F2 on Page CG1) **8.10** £
- Used against gains (total of column K1 on Page CG3, or the smaller of boxes F1 and F2 on Page CG1) **8.11** £
- Used against earlier years' gains (generally only available to personal representatives, see Notes, page CGN11) **8.12** £
- Used against income (only losses of the type described on page CGN9 can be used against income) **8.13A** £ — amount claimed against income of 2001-02 / **8.13B** £ — amount claimed against income of 2000-01 — box 8.13A + box 8.13B **8.13** £
- This year's unused losses — box 8.10 *minus* (boxes 8.11 + 8.12 + 8.13) **8.14** £

■ **Earlier years' losses**

- Unused losses of 1996-97 and later years **8.15** £
- Used this year (losses from box 8.15 are used in priority to losses from box 8.18) (column K3 on Page CG3 or box F6 on Page CG1) **8.16** £
- Remaining unused losses of 1996-97 and later years — box 8.15 *minus* box 8.16 **8.17** £
- Unused losses of 1995-96 and earlier years **8.18** £
- Used this year (losses from box 8.15 are used in priority to losses from box 8.18) (column K3 on Page CG3 or box F6 on Page CG1) — box 8.6 *minus* box 8.16 (or box F6 *minus* box 8.16) **8.19** £

■ **Total of unused losses to carry forward**

- Carried forward losses of 1996-97 and later years — box 8.14 + box 8.17 **8.20** £
- Carried forward losses of 1995-96 and earlier years — box 8.18 *minus* box 8.19 **8.21** £

SPECIMEN

Fig. 24. Page 8 of capital gains pages of self-assessment tax return.

Timing

You may be thinking that it is not always as straightforward and easy to make gains or losses. The above examples show the sorts of circumstances when it is most appropriate to be able to take advantage of the threshold limits.

The approach of the end of the tax year is often the best time to be able to do these sort of transactions. As you approach 5 April you have the choice of whether to carry out transactions before or after that date.

Tax tip
Carrying out transactions before 5 April means that they fall into the present tax year, and could be of use in mitigating this year's tax burden.

It could also be of advantage to postpone transactions until after that date. For instance, you may have made relatively modest gains of, say, £2,000, and you want to carry out another transaction which will show a loss of, say, £1,000. If you did it before 5 April you would reduce a £2,000 gain to a £1,000 gain, and there would be no tax liability in either case. Therefore the loss has been of no practical value to you. If you did it after 5 April the £1,000 loss would be available for the following year, when it might be of use to you.

Trading assets

The other point which becomes obvious is that you have to be able to have assets which will give you the opportunity to trade at a gain or a loss, more or less at will. The assets which are most easily traded are stocks and shares. If you have a portfolio, then there are a variety of stocks and shares, and there may well be some amongst your portfolio which meet the right conditions.

USING THE LOWER RATE BANDS

As we have seen, the rate of Capital Gains Tax depends on the level of Income Tax that you pay. In effect, all of your 'income', whether from income sources or capital gains, are aggregated to arrive at your true tax liability.

Therefore, when considering your capital gains position, you should not look at it in isolation. If you have made a capital gain in a tax year, you should think about your overall tax position. For instance, are there any loss claims you could make against income? Could you make pension contributions? Are there other allowances or reliefs of which you could take advantage? These will all impact upon the Income Tax position, and the effect 'follows through' to the Capital Gains Tax position.

BED AND BREAKFASTING

A method by which you used to be able to take advantage of these provisions was called 'bed and breakfasting'. Unfortunately, it was effectively abolished in the Spring budget of 1998. It involved selling an asset – usually stocks or shares – and buying it back the next day. The sale either established a gain or a loss which was used for the purposes mentioned above. The repurchase the next day meant that it was then deemed to be acquired at the new price for any future capital gains purposes.

Since the Spring budget of 1998, however, any purchases and sales of identical assets within a 30-day period are matched with each other for Capital Gains Tax purposes. The advantage of doing this was therefore lost.

However, there are some options still left open.

- You could sell the shares, and not buy them back for 30 days. This of course greatly increases the risk factor, since the price may have moved adversely in that time.

- You could sell the shares, and repurchase different shares. However, any purchase of shares should be made first and foremost on investment criteria.

- You could sell the shares, and they could be repurchased by your spouse. This, however, would have to be compatible with your overall tax planning, and indeed your overall marriage arrangements.

USING THE RELIEFS

There are a number of reliefs available – some to people in specific circumstances – which can reduce or postpone your Capital Gains Tax liability. Some are deferments only, but it is sometimes possible to defer capital gains almost indefinitely. When you die there is no Capital Gains Tax to pay on whatever passes from your estate to your survivors. Whoever inherits your assets starts off with a clean sheet of the assets at their probate value for Capital Gains Tax purposes.

How do you claim reliefs?
All reliefs are claimed on page 3 of the capital gains pages of your self-assessment tax return (see Figure 22). Claim reliefs in column G, entering the amounts against each individual gain.

ROLLOVER RELIEF

Rollover relief is given to people who are carrying on a business – either alone, in partnership, or a limited company. If you sell any business assets there might be a capital gain liable to tax on the sale. However, if you buy new assets for your business within a certain time limit, the gain may be 'rolled over'. This means that the amount of the

chargeable gain on the asset sold is not assessed to Capital
Gains Tax, but is used to reduce the cost, for Capital Gains
Tax purposes, of the new asset bought. Therefore, if and when
the new asset is eventually sold, the gain on the old asset is
then brought into charge for Capital Gains Tax.

However, the new asset itself may be eligible to roll over
the gain if there is another new asset bought within the time
limit. In this case, the gain from the original asset is rolled
over as well as the gain from the one currently being sold.
The 'rolling over' process can go on without limitation on
the number of times it happens.

Limit on the type of assets

Rollover relief can only be claimed on assets falling within
the following categories:

- land and buildings (including permanent or semi-
  permanent structures in the nature of buildings)
- fixed plant and machinery
- ships, aircraft and hovercraft
- satellites, space stations and spacecraft
- goodwill
- milk quotas, potato quotas and ewe and suckler cow
  premium quotas.

Example
You bought a factory in April 1990 for £50,000. You used it
for your business, then sold it in March 2004 for £110,000.
At the same time you bought a bigger factory for £150,000.
The gain is worked out as follows:

Sale price		110,000
Purchase price	50,000	
Indexation allowance say 30%	15,000	
		65,000
Gain		£ 35,000

146

The rollover relief is given by deducting this chargeable gain of £35,000 from the cost of the new building, ie:

Cost of new building	150,000
Less: gain rolled over	35,000
	£115,000

The new 'base cost' of the new building for Capital Gains Tax purposes is now £115,000.

Question
What if I have received for instance £20,000 for the sale of an asset, but only paid out £15,000 for the replacement asset?

Answer
The gain can only be rolled over in full if the amount spent on the new asset is at least equal to the proceeds of sale of the old asset. Otherwise, the amount of the sale proceeds not used to purchase the new asset remains chargeable to Capital Gains Tax.

Example
Given the same facts as the previous example, except that you bought the new factory for only £90,000, the chargeable gain is the same – £35,000. The amount of the sale price of the old premises which you have not re-invested is £20,000 (ie £110,000 less £90,000).

The amount chargeable to Capital Gains Tax on the sale of the first factory is the lesser of the chargeable gain (£35,000) and the amount not re-invested (£20,000). Therefore £20,000 is charged to Capital Gains Tax.

The cost of the new factory is then reduced by the amount of the gain rolled over, as follows:

Chargeable gain	35,000
Charged to tax	20,000
Amount rolled over	£15,000

The base cost of the new factory then becomes:

Cost of new building	90,000
Less: gain rolled over	15,000
New base cost	£75,000

Time limits
The limit within which the new asset can be bought to qualify for the rollover relief is between one year before and three years after the sale of the first asset.

The normal date for payment of Capital Gains Tax is 31 January following the year of assessment in which the gain was made.

Tax tip
You could have already paid the tax before you purchase a new asset on which the rollover relief can be claimed. In this case you can make the claim and get a refund of the tax you have paid.

TAPER RELIEF

Taper relief replaced both retirement relief and indexation relief from 6 April 1998. It works by reducing the gain chargeable to Capital Gains Tax according to the length of time the assets have been held. There are two scales of taper, one for business assets and one for non-business assets. These scales are as follows:

Number of complete years asset held	*Percentage of gain chargeable*	
	Business assets	*Non-business assets*
less than 1	100%	100%

1	50%	100%
2	25%	100%
3		95%
4		90%
5		85%
6		80%
7		75%
8		70%
9		65%
10 or more		60%

For the purposes of the taper relief, business assets are defined as follows.

Shares

* The company must be a trading company, or the holding company of a trading group.

* The company must be unlisted, or listed on the Alternative Investment Market.

* The individual must have at least 5% of the shares with voting rights in the company.

* The individual must be an officer or employee of the company, or of a company that has a relevant connection with it. If the shares are held by trustees of a settlement, one of the eligible beneficiaries must be an officer or employee of the company.

* Since the 2001 budget, shares held by employees in their employer's company are considered as business assets, even if the company is not a trading company. However, the employee must not have a 'material interest' – which broadly means more than 10% of the shares of the company. This only applies to disposals of these shares after 6 April 2001.

Other assets
An asset of an individual must be used, wholly or partly:

- For a trade carried on by that individual, or by a partnership of which the individual is a member.

- For a trade carried on by a company or a subsidiary of a company in which the individual holds shares which qualify as business assets.

- For an office or employment of a person carrying on a trade.

Trading
It is very important to be able to decide if a company is trading for its shares to qualify for taper relief. The basic definition is:

> *A trading company must exist wholly for the purpose of carrying on one or more trades (apart from any purposes not capable of having any substantial effect on the extent of the company's activities).*

Some things flow from this definition:

- Furnished holiday lettings qualify as a trade.

- A trading group (which consists of a parent company with one or more subsidiaries in which it holds at least 51% of the voting shares) must also meet the same trading definition.

- A company with more than 20% non-trading assets, profits, or activities will fail to qualify as a trading company. Therefore be careful about investing surplus assets or letting surplus property. Even if the property were let to another trading company, it could still disqualify that company as a trading company.

If a company is not a trading company, its shares do not qualify for business taper relief. Even if the company is partly trading and partly non-trading, there is still no provision for apportioning the taper relief; the shares are non-business assets.

Time apportionment

Where an asset has been a business asset for part of the period of ownership, and a non-business asset for the rest, there are complex rules for apportioning the gain chargeable to Capital Gains Tax.

- First, the use of the asset taken into account is the shorter of
  – the ten years ending with the disposal, or
  – the period after 5 April 1998.
  This is known as the 'relevant period of ownership'.

- Then the length of time for which the asset was used for a business purpose is taken as a proportion of the total length of the relevant period of ownership.

- Business taper relief is given on this proportion.

- Non-business taper relief is given on the rest.

- Taper relief is calculated separately on the two elements by reference to the 'relevant period of ownership'.

This creates an anomaly. An asset could have been used for a business purpose for the last four years before its disposal, but for a non-business purpose before that. In this case the maximum business taper relief would not be available. Since 6 April 2000 there were some changes in the rules which could give rise to these apportionments. These include some shares which did not qualify before 6 April 2000 but did qualify after that date; an employee leaving a listed company but retaining shares; a property which starts or

ceases to be used for a trade; a company going into
liquidation and ceasing to trade.

Example
An asset was used for three years after 5 April 1998 as a
non-business asset, then for two years as a business asset. It
is disposed of, giving rise to a gain of £10,000. If it were a
business asset, held for two years, the whole of the £10,000
would be eligible for the 75% reduction. But because it had
some prior non-business use only 40% – ie £4,000 – is
eligible for the 75% reduction. The other £6,000 qualifies
for the non-business reduction of 40%, leaving 60%
chargeable. The total reduction is therefore £5,400,
compared to £7,500 if it had been a business asset for the
whole of the period.

Tax tip
So what can be done about this anomaly? If you have an
asset which has been a non-business asset, but which will
start being used as a business asset, you could re-start the
clock by transferring the asset into a trust in which you
have an interest. This will obviously need a solicitor's help.
The gain on the transfer into the trust would be held over,
but the trust's taper relief would start on the date of the
transfer, and therefore remove the non-business period. The
trustees would then hold the asset for at least four years to
get the maximum relief.

HOLD OVER RELIEF

Hold over relief applies to gifts or transfers of business
assets or agricultural property 'not at arm's length'. A
transaction 'not at arm's length' means one where the
transaction is between 'connected persons' and therefore not
at a full market value. The definition of 'connected

persons' is looked at in Chapter 13 in more detail.

Hold over relief operates in a similar way to rollover relief as described above. In other words, the gain is 'held over' until the person acquiring the asset disposes of it. In order to get the relief, both the person making the transfer and the person receiving it must make a joint claim. This claim can be made for assets used in a business, shares in a trading company, or agricultural property.

A common scenario

The most common scenario for this claim is a person passing on a business to someone in their family by gifting the whole business, or assets of the business, to that other person. Although the person receiving the gift has received it free, he or she will have to bear the ultimate Capital Gains Tax liability, unless they in turn pass it on to somebody else.

Warning
If the person receiving the gift or transfer becomes non-resident in the UK there is a clawback of the relief.

DEFERRING THE GAIN

There are two schemes which enable you to defer a capital gain. They also have other important incentives, which apply for Income Tax purposes.

Enterprise Investment Scheme

Any chargeable gain you make may be deferred by reinvesting in the **Enterprise Investment Scheme** (EIS). The gain is then deferred until a chargeable event arises. This is normally the sale of the EIS shares. However, when this occurs the gain can then be deferred again by further reinvestment.

To qualify for this scheme there are several conditions which you must meet.

- You must subscribe for newly-issued ordinary shares – you cannot buy shares for this scheme.

- The company must be an unquoted company. However, the company may be quoted on the AIM (Alternative Investment Market).

- The company must be a trading company. There are a number of activities which disqualify it as a trading company. These include:
  - money lending, banking, insurance
  - hire purchase financing
  - dealing in land, commodities, futures, shares, or financial instruments
  - accountancy or legal services
  - leasing or receiving royalties or licence fees
  - farming
  - forestry and timber production
  - market gardening
  - operating or managing hotels or guest houses
  - residential care nursing homes.

- The investment must be made within the period starting one year before and ending three years after the date of the original gain.

- There is no minimum or maximum limit to investments to qualify for the deferral relief. However, there may be limits on investments in any one individual company.

- You may invest in your own company and still get deferral relief.

Withdrawal of the relief
The relief is withdrawn if the shares cease to be qualifying

shares, or the company ceases to be a trading company.

Some of the conditions which must be met for the investment to qualify for income tax relief do not necessarily have to apply for the deferral of Capital Gains Tax relief.

Venture Capital Trusts

Capital gains may also be deferred by reinvesting in a Venture Capital Trust (VCT). This is a fully quoted public company similar to an investment trust company. It invests in other companies, but in order to qualify for the deferral relief (and the Income Tax relief) the companies in which it invests must be non-quoted companies.

As with EIS shares the shares cannot be bought to get the relief, but they must be new ordinary shares subscribed for. The other conditions are broadly similar to the conditions for EIS shares. The qualification of being a trading company relates to the unquoted companies in which the VCT invests.

An important difference, however, is in the time limit. To get the deferral relief the reinvestment in VCT shares must be made between one year before and one year after the date of the original gain.

TAX EFFICIENCY AUDIT

1. Do you know how much gain you have made for Capital Gains Tax purposes when you sell shares?

2. Do you have surplus allowances or lower rate tax bands available?

3. Do you have any assets on which you could establish a loss?

4. Are you thinking of selling your business? If so, have you thought about the timing implications?

5. If you are thinking of passing your business to the next generation of your family, could you benefit from hold over relief?

6. Can you reinvest any proceeds of sale of assets – either into more business assets for rollover relief, or into Enterprise Investment Scheme or Venture Capital Trusts to defer the gain?

9

Rewarding Employees

If you have employees you will want to offer them the best
possible rewards. This involves paying them in the most tax
efficient way – both for you and for them. Always
remember, if you are a director of a limited company you
are also an employee of that company.

OPERATING PAYE

If you have any employees working for you, you must
operate a PAYE system. This is the means by which you, the
employer, collect Income Tax and National Insurance from
the employee on behalf of the Inland Revenue, and then pay
it over to the Inland Revenue. The system is also used to pay
statutory sick pay, statutory maternity pay, working families
tax credit, and to collect repayments of student loans. You
must register with your local Inland Revenue office, who
will give you a PAYE reference number.

The system is operated by paperwork which the Inland
Revenue supply. They also carry out training on operating
the PAYE system, by having occasional workshops.
However, the paperwork for operating the PAYE system
does come with a complete guide, and you can learn the
system by reading it. Many self-employed people, however,
seek the help and advice of their accountant either to
operate the system for them, or to get them started. There
are also various software packages which enable you to
computerise your PAYE operation.

Operating the system

If you take on an employee, they should have a P45 (see Figure 25) from their previous employment. This tells you when they left the employment, their tax code, the total gross earnings up to the time they left and the tax deducted up to that date. You will use this as the start of your records.

If the employee does not have a P45, ask them to fill in a form P46 (see Figure 26). This tells you whether this employment is their only or main employment, or if they are a student, etc. If they cannot certify any of these categories you must apply an emergency code, and ask the Tax Office to supply a code notice for this employee.

The basic form for deducting tax and National Insurance is the P11 (see Figure 27). You must keep a separate form for each employee.

Calculating Income Tax

The basic tool for operating the tax system is the code number. Each employee has their own code number. This number is the starting point for working through tables to find out how much Income Tax the employee has to pay on the weekly or monthly pay. Income Tax is calculated on a cumulative basis. This means that the Income Tax is calculated on the total earnings since the beginning of the tax year, then you deduct what has been paid so far. This is why there are sometimes refunds of tax, following a change of code or a gap in pay.

Calculating National Insurance

National Insurance is not calculated on a cumulative basis (except for company directors). You simply read off the amount of National Insurance to pay on that week's or that month's pay from the tables. If the employee is below the limit for any week or month there is no National Insurance to deduct, but there is no carry forward to the next week or month. There are two elements to National Insurance:

When detaching a page, please leave this stub intact on the remaining pages.

Inland **Revenue**

Details of employee leaving work | **P45**
Copy for Tax Office | **Part 1**

1 PAYE Reference

Office number   Reference number

2 Employee's National Insurance number

(Mr Mrs Miss Ms Other)

3 Surname (in capitals)

First name(s) (in capitals)

4 Leaving date (in figures)
Day   Month   Year

5 Continue Student Loan Deductions(Y)

6 Tax Code at leaving date. *If Week 1 or Month 1 basis applies, write 'X' in the box marked* Week 1 or Month 1
Code   Week 1 or Month 1

7 Last entries on *Deductions Working Sheet (P11)* **Complete only if Tax Code is cumulative.** *Make no entry here if Week 1 or Month 1 basis applies. Go to item 8.*

Week or month number   Week   Month

Total pay to date £   p

Total tax to date £   p

8 This employment pay and tax. ■ *No entry needed if Tax Code is cumulative and amounts are same as item 7 entries*

Total pay in this employment £   p

Total tax in this employment £   p

9 Works number/ Payroll number

10 Department or branch if any

11 Employee's private address and Postcode

12 I certify that the details entered above in items 1 to 10 are correct

Employer's name, address and Postcode

Date

To the employer   *Please complete with care* ★

For Tax Office use

- Complete this form following the 'Employee leaving' instructions in the *Employer's Quick Guide to PAYE and NICs* (cards CWG1). ★ **Make sure the details are clear on all four parts of this form.** Make sure your name and address is shown on Parts 1 and 1A.
- Detach Part 1 and send it to your Tax Office immediately.
- Hand Parts 1A, 2 and 3 (unseparated) to your employee when he or she leaves.
- If the employee has died, write 'D' in this box and send all four parts of this form (unseparated) to your Tax Office immediately.

P45   BMSD9/99

Fig. 25. P45 form.

159

PAYE Employer's notice to Inland Revenue Office

Send in on the first pay day for employees who
- *do not have a form P45, or*
- *were previously paid below the PAYE threshold.*

Inland Revenue

Section 1 - to be completed by the EMPLOYEE

Read each statement carefully. Tick **each one** that applies to you. **If none of them apply, do not sign the statement.**

Statement A
This is my first regular job since leaving full-time education. I have not claimed
Jobseeker's Allowance, or income support paid because of unemployment since then. ☐

Statement B
This is my only or main job. ☐

Statement C
I receive a pension as well as the income from this job. ☐

I confirm that I have ticked the statements that apply to me.

Signed _____ Date ____/____/____

Section 2 - to be completed by the EMPLOYER

Your employer's Quick Guide to PAYE and NICs (CWG1, card 5) tells you how to complete this form.

Employee's details

National Insurance number ☐☐ ☐☐ ☐☐ ☐☐ ☐

Surname including title Mr/Mrs/Miss/Ms/Other
_____

First name(s)
_____

Address
_____
_____
_____
_____ Postcode _____

Date of birth ____/____/____

Male/Female (*enter M/F*) ☐

Works/payroll number, if any _____

Department/Branch, if any _____

Job title _____

Date employment started ____/____/____

Coding information

Existing employee now above PAYE threshold
(*enter X in box if this applies*) ☐

New employee who has signed statement (*enter letter here*) ☐

New employee who has not signed a statement ☐

Code operated for this employee _____

Enter X in box if code operated on week1/month 1 basis ☐

Employer's details

Employer's PAYE reference _____

Name _____

Address
_____
_____
_____
_____ Postcode _____

Date this form was completed ____/____/____

P46   BMSD11/99

Fig. 26. P46 form.

160

Deductions Working Sheet P11 Year to 5 April **2002**

Employee's details *In CAPITALS*

Box A Employer's name

Box C Surname

Box B Inland Revenue office and Employer s PAYE reference

Box D First two forenames

Notes:

1 For guidance on earnings, *National Insurance* and *completing columns 1a to 1i*, see *Employer's Help Cards*.
For guidance on *Statutory Sick Pay* figures, see booklet *CA30* ; and for *Statutory Maternity Pay* figures, see booklet *CA29*.
For guidance on *Student Loan Deductions*, see *Card 22* of *Employer's Help Cards*.

If you need further assistance, please contact the Employer's Helpline on 0845 7 143 143.

2 *In the NI Tables, a letter is shown at the top of each section, for example A, B, C, D or E. Copy the Table Letter you use to the Table Letter box in the* **End of Year Summary** *overleaf. If the employee's circumstances change part way through a year, the Table Letter may change as well. Record all Table Letters used and enter separate totals for each one.*

National Insurance contributions Note: LEL = *Lower Earnings Limit*, UEL = *Upper Earnings Limit*

Month no	Week no	For Employer s use	Earnings at the LEL (where earnings are equal to or exceed the LEL) 1a £	Earnings above the LEL, up to and including the Earnings Threshold 1b £	Earnings above the Earnings Threshold, up to and including the UEL 1c £	Total of employee's and employer s contributions payable 1d £ p	Employee's contributions payable on earnings in 1c (before deducting ... NIC rebate ... 1e £ p	Employee s NIC rebate due on earnings ... to be deducted from contributions in 1e) 1f £ p	Emplo... due on and ar emplo due bu in 1f 1g
	1								
	2								
	3								
1	4								
	5								
2	6								
	7								
	8								
	9								
	10								
	11								
3	12								
	13								
	14								
	15								
	16								
4	17								
	18								
	19								
	20								
5	21								
	22								
	23								
	24								
	25								
6	26								
	27								
	28								
	29								
7	30								
			Total c/fwd	Total c/fwd	Total c/fwd	Total c/fwd	Total c/fwd	Total c/fwd	

SPECIMEN

P11(2001)

BMSD 11/00

Fig. 27. P11 form.

161

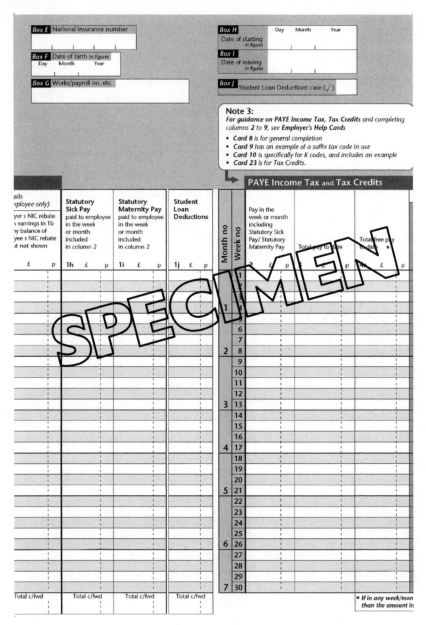

Fig. 27. (continued).

162

Please keep this form for at least 3 years after the end of the year
to which it relates, or longer if you are asked to do so.

Box K Tax code †	† If amended cross out previous code	Box M		Tax Credits				
		If authorised to make payments to employee, you can record start, daily rate and stop details here. Record amounts paid to employee in column 9.						
		Start Date			Daily Rate		Stop Date	
Box L Amended code †	Wk/Mth in which applied	Day Month Year			£ p		Day Month Year	

K codes only				K codes only			K codes only	Tax Credits
Total additional pay to date (Table A)	Total taxable pay to date i.e. column 3 *minus* column 4a or column 3 *plus* column 4b ★	Total tax due to date as shown by Taxable Pay Tables	Tax due at end of current period *Mark refunds R*	Regulatory limit i.e. 50% of column 2 entry	Tax deducted or refunded in the week or month *Mark refunds R*	Tax not deducted owing to the Regulatory		
4b £ p	5 £ p	6 £ p	6a £ p	6b £ p	7 p	8	9 £ p

…th the amount in column 4a is more
…n column 3, leave column 5 blank.

Total c/fwd

Fig. 27. (continued).

- The employer's contribution is a cost that you, the employer, have to bear.

- The employee's contribution is deducted from their pay.

Directors' National Insurance
National Insurance is calculated by reference to a 'pay period'. This is usually determined as the normal period for which employees are paid – usually weekly or monthly. However, directors are always treated on a yearly basis (ie their pay period is annual). This means that the calculation of Directors' National Insurance is done on a cumulative basis. If a director is paid monthly the actual cumulative pay each month is compared to the annual limit for National Insurance, and divided by 12. It often happens, therefore, that for the first few months of the tax year directors pay no National Insurance. By the end of the year, though, it catches up.

Paying over the tax
You must pay over the tax and National Insurance deducted (and your employer's contribution of National Insurance) to the Inland Revenue. Depending on the size of your PAYE bill, you pay this over monthly or quarterly. This is money which you are holding on behalf of the Inland Revenue for your employees. The Inland Revenue therefore take this debt very seriously – more seriously, in fact, than ordinary Income Tax or Corporation Tax. They will press harder for collection if you are in default, and the debt is a preferential debt if you are in bankruptcy or liquidation.

End of year returns
At the end of each tax year you, the employer, must send in a return to the Inland Revenue of all the tax and National Insurance deductions for each employee. You must also supply each employee with a certificate (a P60) showing their

total earnings for the tax year, the total National Insurance contributions, and the total tax deducted. You must also supply a form P11D to each employee who is eligible.

A form P11D is a statement of benefits received by the employee, and expenses reimbursed to the employee. The employee will need this to complete their tax return, so it is important to supply this within the time limit.

Enquiries
The Inland Revenue carry out periodic audits into employers and their compliance with PAYE regulations. If you are informed of a PAYE audit, don't panic! The Inland Revenue Inspector will be looking in your accounting records for evidence of payments or benefits to people who you should have been including in your PAYE system.

Penalties and interest
It is important to get it right. Although you act as an unpaid tax collector for the government, there are penalties and interest for not sending in the paperwork on time, and especially for not paying over the money deducted from employees.

EMPLOYING YOUR SPOUSE

Small business owners often employ their spouses in their business. We have seen in Chapter 5 that there can be advantages in having your spouse as a business partner rather than an employee. If your business is a limited company it is often advantageous for your spouse to be a director (and sometimes secretary) of the company.

Employing your spouse is no different in principle to employing anybody else. You must observe the same regulations relating to the national minimum wage, for example. You must also operate the PAYE system in the same way as for anybody else. Perhaps most obvious is the need to actually pay your spouse, and record the transaction. It has not been unknown for the owner of a small business to see his accountant at the end of the year, and say something like 'How have we done this year? OK, let's put in wages for my wife, say £3,000.'

In order for this to be a valid deduction against profits it must actually be paid, and recorded. It must also have the PAYE system applied to it. However, the wages may be paid up to nine months after the end of the accounting period, and still be deducted from the profits for that accounting period.

EMPLOYEES' STATUS

Owners of small businesses are very often faced with the problem of the status of the people who work for them. Sometimes a person will claim to be self-employed, and you may be tempted to take them on on that basis because it seems a lot less hassle. But the Inland Revenue do not always agree to that without enquiring further. This sort of problem often crops up during a PAYE audit.

If they suspect that a person is really an employee they will apply certain tests, and the person concerned will be under enquiry as well as yourself. Here are some of the guidelines they use to determine whether a person is employed or self-employed:

- Who calls the shots? Do you, the employer, say when they must work, and under what conditions?

- Do they work substantially for one person? If so, that would be an indication of employment rather than self-employment.

- Do they supply their own tools or equipment? If not,

that is another indication of employment rather than self-employment.

- Do they take any degree of commercial risk? If so, that is an indication of self-employment.

- Can they delegate their work to someone else in their absence? If not, they are probably employed rather than self-employed.

All of these tests are considered separately, and together they build up a body of evidence which the Inland Revenue use to decide a person's status. If the balance is towards employment, they can work out the Income Tax and National Insurance you should have paid and demand that from you, the employer. It is then up to you to try to recoup that money from the employee.

You can, of course, appeal against this decision, but be prepared to fight the case before the Commissioners.

BENEFITS FOR EMPLOYEES

You can reward your employees, and yourself if you are a director, by benefits in kind as well as a salary. In general the taxation charge on a benefit is equal to the actual value of that benefit. At the end of each tax year the employer must provide the employee with a form P11D to show the value of all benefits provided. The employee then uses that as the basis of their entry on their tax return for benefits received. The employer, besides supplying this to the employee, also has to supply it to the Inland Revenue as part of the end of year PAYE return. So the Inland Revenue can always check up on the benefits figures of employees.

However, for motor cars the benefit is a fixed percentage of the price when new of the car, adjusted for the amount of business mileage travelled. This can prove expensive to the employee, particularly if the business mileage is low. However, the basis for the benefit charge for the future will be the fuel efficiency of the car. If fuel is provided by the employer for the employee's private mileage there are further scale charges according to the size of the engine, and whether it is diesel or petrol fuelled.

A recent concession was that the loan of a computer (with a value up to £2,000) by an employer to an employee is exempt from tax.

Tax tip
Computer equipment qualifies for 100% first year capital allowances. The employer can therefore buy a computer (up to £2,000) which is loaned to the employee, and claim the full cost against tax. The employee does not suffer any tax on this benefit.

A few years later the employee could buy the computer at its market value (and we all know how rapidly computer values diminish), and thus has acquired a computer very cheaply. This could perhaps be done when the employer was going to update the equipment anyway. However, proper records must be kept to verify this whole transaction.

Some companies are giving more benefits these days, and the ways in which they are granted can be very flexible. For instance, the employer can offer a total value of benefits (say 10% of salary) which the employee can choose how he 'spends'. Thus the employee might be able to choose from a whole menu of benefits including things like life assurance, childcare, healthcare, private medical insurance and so on.

Home working
Employers may now contribute towards additional home expenses incurred by employees working some or all of their time at home under agreed flexible working arrangements. This will not give rise to a tax or National Insurance charge.

Employers may pay up to £2 per week without the need for any supporting evidence. Above that figure, however, evidence is needed to support the claim that the payment is wholly for additional expenses incurred by the employee in carrying out his duties at home.

SHARE SCHEME INCENTIVES

If you own a limited company you may be able to benefit yourself and your employees by share scheme incentives.

For your employees this sort of scheme is useful as a 'golden handcuff'. It rewards them for performance, gives them a chance to benefit from future growth of the company, and gives them a reason to identify with the company. It thus promotes loyalty, and discourages employees from leaving when their incentives may be lost.

Under share schemes, you may enable employees to acquire shares by:

- issuing free shares, or
- allowing employees to buy shares at less than the full market value, or
- granting an option to buy the shares at a fixed or discounted price at some future date.

You must, of course, be enabled to carry out such a scheme by the Memorandum and Articles of Association of the company. You should also make absolutely sure that you do not breach the Financial Services Act. Any such breach is a *criminal* offence. You could breach this Act by recommending the company's shares as an investment to your employees.

If an employee has benefited from any arrangement which gives rise to an Income Tax charge they must complete the 'share schemes' pages of the self-assessment tax return.

Share schemes may be approved or unapproved by the Inland Revenue. Approved schemes benefit from tax advantages, but are generally less flexible.

Unapproved schemes

If the schemes are unapproved they may be subject to tax and National Insurance in the following circumstances:

- If the employee buys the shares at less than their market value Income Tax is charged on the difference between the market value and the amount actually paid. National Insurance can also be payable if the shares are 'readily convertible'. That means that the shares are quoted on a stock exchange, or arrangements exist to enable the employee to sell the shares for cash.

- If payment for the shares is deferred Income Tax and National Insurance are payable. The deferral is treated as a loan, and the benefit in kind rules apply. Therefore if the employee's salary plus the value of this benefit does not exceed £8,500 a year, there is no tax or National Insurance charge.

- If the shares are acquired through the exercise of an option, tax is charged on the difference between the market value of the shares and the amount paid under the option, plus the amount paid (if any) for the option.

National Insurance is only payable if the shares are 'readily convertible', as defined above.

- If the option can be granted more than ten years after it is granted, Income Tax is charged on the grant of the option. Tax is charged on the difference between the market price of the shares when the option is granted, and the price to be paid for the shares when the option is exercised, plus the amount paid (if any) for the option. When tax is paid under these provisions, it can be deducted from any tax payable when the employee exercises the option.

National Insurance is only payable if the shares are 'readily convertible' as defined above.

- If shares acquired under an unapproved scheme are subsequently sold at a profit they are subject to Capital Gains Tax in the normal way. The tax is charged on:
  - the amount realised from the sale of the shares, less
  - the amount paid for the shares, plus
  - the amount paid for the option, plus
  - the amount taxed as income under any of the above provisions, plus
  - indexation allowance (where applicable), plus
  - taper relief (where applicable).

- Tax can also be charged under other circumstances, including:
  - If there are arrangements to artificially boost the value of shares, such as the removal of a restriction.
  - If the shares are in a 51% subsidiary which trades significantly with other members of the same group of companies.
  - If the shareholder receives a special benefit.
  - If the shares are subject to forfeiture, and the forfeiture is lifted.
  - If the shares are converted into shares of another class with an increase in the market value.

Approved schemes
There are four types of Inland Revenue approved share schemes.

1. All-employee share ownership plan (aesop).

2. Savings-related share option scheme.

3. Approved company share option scheme.

4. Enterprise management incentive share scheme.

   The first three of these must have formal Inland Revenue approval before the tax advantages are granted.

How do you get approval?
The approval must be obtained from the Inland Revenue Share Schemes department, at Room 76, New Wing, Somerset House, London WC2R 1LB.

   For the first two of these schemes the employee may not participate if he or she (together with associates) can control (directly or indirectly) at least 25% of the ordinary shares of the company. Similar rules apply to the other two schemes, but the limit figure is 10% for scheme number 3, and 30% for scheme number 4.

   All four plans can include employees of a company controlled by the scheme company, as well as employees of the company itself.

All-employee share ownership plan
This scheme may be set up by almost any company. Exceptions are companies which exist wholly or mainly to provide services to an associated company or to the persons who control the company. The scheme must allow all employees (full-time or part-time) of the company to participate on equal terms, but:

*   Shares may be issued free or for payment from salary (before tax).

*   The company may allocate benefits linked to salary, length of service, or hours worked.

*   The company may impose a qualifying length of service

to join the scheme of up to 18 months, although this period cannot be varied for different classes of employees.

- Employees may only receive free shares under one scheme, so they cannot also be granted free shares under an approved profit-sharing scheme.

There are certain limits to the issue of shares under this scheme.

1. The company may give any employee free shares up to a market value of £3,000 in any one year. Some or all of these free shares may be awarded to employees for performance-related achievements.

2. Employees may buy 'partnership shares' up to 10% of their salary (before tax and National Insurance), up to a maximum of £1,500 a year.

3. The company may give up to two 'matching shares' to each employee for each 'partnership share' purchased by the employee. These shares must be given free, and must be provided to all members on the same basis.

4. Employees may reinvest up to £1,500 per year of dividends received on the shares in new shares. This must be done within 30 days of receiving the dividend.

5. All shares must be held within a trust specially set up for this purpose.

6. Free shares and 'matching shares' must be held within the trust for a minimum period of time determined by the company. This minimum may be between three and five years.

7. Employees may withdraw 'partnership shares' from the trust at any time.

8. Shares acquired by reinvestment of dividends must be held in the trust for at least three years.

9. When the employee leaves the employment of the company, he or she must withdraw the shares from the trust.

10. The company may forfeit free shares or matching shares if an employee leaves the company within a set period, which cannot be longer than three years. However, shares may not be forfeited when the cause of leaving the company is injury, disability, redundancy, retirement, death, or changes in the control of the company.

11. A company may not make any loans to employees in this plan.

The tax advantages are as follows:

*   No tax is charged on shares given or bought up to the limits imposed.

*   If free shares or matching shares are withdrawn before three years, Income Tax is charged on the market value of the shares at the date of withdrawal, less any amount paid for the shares.

*   If free or matching shares are withdrawn between three and five years, Income Tax is charged on the lower of the market value at the date of withdrawal or the market value at the date the shares were given.

*   If dividend shares are withdrawn within three years, tax is charged on the original dividend, but in the tax year when the shares are withdrawn.

*   All withdrawals of shares after five years are free of tax.

*   Any growth in the value of the shares while they are in the plan is free of Capital Gains Tax. If shares are

withdrawn they are only liable to Capital Gains Tax on the growth in value after they are withdrawn.

- When shares are withdrawn from the plan they may be transferred into an ISA, or into a stakeholder pension, subject to the normal limits. This must be done within 90 days of withdrawing them from the plan.

- The company can deduct from its profits the cost of operating the plan, and the market value of free and matching shares when they are put into the trust.

Savings-related share option schemes
These are plans linked to **Save As You Earn (SAYE)** contracts. However, the employees do not have to take up shares under the SAYE contracts. They may simply withdraw the cash proceeds of the SAYE scheme tax-free.

The employer must allow all employees (full-time and part-time) to participate on equal terms. Part-time directors, however, may be excluded. The employer may impose a qualifying period of employment for membership of the scheme. For this scheme the period may be up to five years. The conditions of the scheme must include the following:

1. Under the SAYE contract employees must save between £5 and £250 per month with a recognised bank, building society or other authorised financial institution.

2. The SAYE scheme must be for three or five years. Five year schemes must have the option to extend to seven years. At the end of the period of the contract a bonus is paid.

3. Shares may be bought with the proceeds of the SAYE savings, under an option scheme. The price at which the shares may be bought must be stated, and must not be less than 80% of the market value of the shares when the option is granted.

4. Options should not be able to be exercised before the bonus date under the SAYE scheme. However, options may be exercised early in the case of death, or where the employee has left the employment due to injury, disability, retirement or redundancy. In these cases the option must be exercised within six months (or 12 months in the case of death).

5. Apart from the above exceptions, the options lapse when an employee leaves employment within three years.

6. If employees leave employment after three years they may exercise the option within six months of leaving. If the employee remains employed by an associated company of the company that set up the scheme, they may exercise the option within six months from the bonus date.

7. If the company is taken over the scheme may allow options to be exchanged for options in the new company.

8. The shares which are the subject of the option must be fully paid up, without any restrictions, and open ended (ie not redeemable).

The tax advantages are as follows:

- For options exercised after at least three years there is no Income Tax charged on the grant of the option, or on the exercise of the option.

- No tax is charged on any increase in the value of the shares between the grant of the option and the exercise of the option.

- When the shares are acquired their base cost for Capital Gains Tax purposes is the amount paid for the shares under the option, plus the amount paid for the option (if any).

- The taper relief period for Capital Gains Tax starts on the date of the exercise of the option.

- Interest and bonuses under the SAYE scheme are tax-free.

Approved company share option plan
Under this scheme employers may offer options to employees to buy shares at the market value when the option is granted at any time between three and ten years after the option is granted. This scheme does not have to be open to all employees. Companies often use it to reward directors or senior employees.

The following is a summary of the conditions:

1. There is a maximum value of £30,000 for any one individual under this scheme.

2. The scheme cannot include part-time directors (part-time is defined for these purposes as being less than 25 hours per week).

3. If the scheme was approved before 1 May 1995 part-time employees cannot participate (unless the rules have been specifically changed for this provision after 1 May 1995).

4. Options may only be exercised within three years if the employee dies within that time.

5. If the option has not been taken up after ten years, it lapses.

6. An employee may not exercise the option more than once every three years.

7. The price at which the shares may be bought under the option must be fixed at the time of the option, and must not be less than the market value of the shares at that time.

8. The shares which are the subject of the option must be fully paid up, without any restrictions, and open ended (ie not redeemable).

The tax advantages are as follows:

- No tax is charged on the grant of the option. However, if the price fixed for the shares turns out to be less than the market value of the shares at that time, the difference is taxable.

- No tax is charged on the exercise of the option.

- No tax is charged on any increase in value of the shares between the date of the grant of the option and the date it is exercised.

- The base cost of the shares for Capital Gains Tax purposes is the amount paid for the shares under the option, plus the amount paid for the option (if any).

- The taper relief period for Capital Gains Tax starts on the date of the exercise of the option.

- The costs of setting up the scheme are tax deductible for the company.

Enterprise management incentive share scheme
This scheme is more flexible than the approved company share option scheme. It allows a company to grant options to up to 15 key employees. To benefit from this scheme you do not have to get advance approval from the Inland Revenue. There is no restriction of the price at which options are granted.

The following is a summary of the conditions:

1. The options must be capable of being exercised within ten years.

2. Up to 15 employees may hold options at any one time.

3. To qualify the employee must not hold more than 30% of the shares of the company (either alone or with associates).

4. The employee must work at least 25 hours per week for the company. However, there is an exception to this. If the employee works at least 75% of their total working time on the business of the company, a total of less than 25 hours per week is permitted.

5. There must be a commercial reason for granting the options. This can include recruitment or retention of key employees, but it cannot be simply for the tax advantage.

6. The company must not be a 51% subsidiary of another company, or under the control of another company in any other way.

7. The company must not have any subsidiaries of its own, where it controls less than 75% of the subsidiary.

8. The gross assets of the company must not exceed £15 million.

9. The main purpose of the company must be to carry on one of the qualifying trades, and it must actually be trading or preparing to trade.

10. The qualifying trades must be carried on wholly or mainly in the UK, on a commercial basis. The qualifying trades are substantially the same as those for Enterprise Investment Relief (see Chapter 8).

11. The shares must be fully paid up ordinary shares, not redeemable. However, they may be subject to restrictions or forfeiture if, for example, certain targets or achievements are not met.

12. An employee may hold options which they have not yet

exercised up to £100,000 in value. They may exercise options if they have reached this limit and then be granted new options. However, the overall time limit of three years must be observed for exercising the options, whether new or existing ones. The new options must not be granted within three years of the original ones. If there is any excess over £100,000, the status of the first £100,000 is not affected. It is only the excess which is invalid.

13. In reckoning the £100,000 above, any options not yet exercised in a company share option plan must also be counted in.

14. The company and the employee must jointly give notice to the Inland Revenue that the requirements of the Enterprise Management Incentive Scheme have been met. This notice must be in the prescribed form (which the Inland Revenue will provide, or which can be obtained from the Inland Revenue website) and it must be made within 30 days of any option being granted.

15. Where the company or the employee break any of the conditions (for example if the employee leaves), the option must be exercised within 40 days, or it becomes invalid.

16. If the company is taken over the options may be replaced by options in the new company, but only if it meets basically the same conditions.

The tax advantages are as follows:

- No tax is charged on the grant of the option, even if it is capable of being exercised after ten years.

- When the option is exercised, Income Tax is charged on the difference between the amount paid for the shares and the market value of the shares at the time the option was granted.

- The base cost for Capital Gains Tax purposes is the

amount paid under the option plus any amount on which Income Tax was charged when the option was exercised.

- The taper relief period for Capital Gains Tax starts on the date the option was granted.

- If an option is disqualified for any reason, any increase in the market value of the shares between the date of the grant of the option and the date of disqualification is free of Income Tax.

- The costs of setting up the scheme are tax deductible for the company.

Share valuation

The valuation of shares in the employer company is obviously a key element in any share option scheme. The valuation of shares in a small company is much more difficult than shares in a quoted company. The Inland Revenue has a share valuation division which deals exclusively with share valuations, for these purposes and for Capital Gains Tax purposes.

The actual process of agreeing a valuation of shares can be long and drawn out, particularly if there is a dispute. The basic question which determines the value of shares is 'How much would a willing buyer be prepared to pay in an open market for these shares?'. To answer this question, all the circumstances of the shares need to be looked at. Perhaps most influential is the record of the company's profits, and its past dividend record. Prices of shares in similar companies quoted on stock exchanges will serve as a guide, but those prices must be heavily discounted to reflect the non-marketability of small companies' shares. A further consideration is whether the shares concerned are a majority holding or a minority holding. In small companies, particularly family companies, this distinction is quite critical.

TAX EFFICIENCY AUDIT

1. Are you confident that you are operating the PAYE system correctly? Do you need any help understanding it? Where would you go for that help?

2. If you and your spouse work together in the business, are you doing so in the most tax-efficient manner?

3. Have you correctly classified everybody who does work for you as employed or self-employed? Are you sure of the guidelines to determine this?

4. If your business is a limited company, have you considered any of the share schemes and incentives – both for yourself as director and for your staff?

10

Inheritance Tax

'In this world, nothing can be said to be certain except death and taxes.'

Benjamin Franklin

Inheritance Tax is one that does not strike until you have died, so it may seem unnecessary to plan to pay less. However, this tax strikes at your dependants. Therefore, unless you really want the Inland Revenue to inherit some of your estate, at the expense of your survivors, you ought to think about this tax.

Inheritance Tax is payable on death, at a rate of 40% on any of your estate that exceeds £255,000. The first £255,000 is at a nil rate (at the time of writing).

LIFETIME TRANSFERS

There is also a lower rate of tax (20%) on some transfers of assets during your lifetime. The transfers which are caught by this tax are transfers into a **discretionary trust**. Again, however, the first £255,000 is at a nil rate, and only the excess over £255,000 is taxed at 20%.

A discretionary trust is one by which the trustees have discretion to make payments of income out of the trust, and also to decide the shares of the capital of the trust each potential beneficiary will receive.

There is also a periodical tax charge on these trusts every ten years, and an 'exit' tax charge when a distribution of capital is made from the trust.

Inheritance Tax on death

The tax is charged on the value of all assets of the deceased, if he or she is domiciled in the UK. If domiciled outside the UK (see Chapter 4), the tax is only charged on assets situated in the UK. It is also charged on gifts or transfers made during the seven years before death. However, assets passing to the spouse of the deceased are exempt from this tax. If you die leaving a spouse, therefore, anything you leave him or her is free of tax. However, anything else left to anybody else, including other members of your family, is liable to the tax if your estate is over £255,000.

POTENTIALLY EXEMPT TRANSFERS

Transfers of value can be made without any liability as long as the donor survives seven years after making them. Potentially exempt transfers are any gifts or transfers made to:

- another individual
- an 'interest in possession' trust
- an 'accumulation and maintenance' trust
- or a trust for a mentally or physically disabled person.

Any transfers or gifts not falling within these categories are chargeable transfers.

How do you claim relief for potentially exempt transfers?
To claim the relief of a potentially exempt transfer, it is important to keep as full records as possible about your financial transactions. Thus, when you die and your executor comes to sort out your estate, they will have records of the dates and persons to whom you have made transfers.

Tapering the relief

If a person has made one or more potentially exempt transfers, and dies within the seven years, the value of the gift or transfer is brought into the estate, but the tax on them is reduced by the following table:

Number of complete years since the gift was made	Percentage of tax payable on death
Not more than 3	100%
More than 3 but less than 4	80%
More than 4 but less than 5	60%
More than 5 but less than 6	40%
More than 6 but less than 7	20%
More than 7	Nil

EXEMPT TRANSFERS

Apart from the potentially exempt transfers, some transfers or gifts are exempt without any qualification. These can therefore be used as a tool to pay less Inheritance Tax. The exempt transfers are as follows.

Transfers between husband and wife

We have already seen that anything passing between husband and wife at death is exempt. Anything passing between husband and wife during lifetime is also exempt. There are a couple of points to note, however.

1. This exemption only applies to husband and wife. Unmarried people living together do not qualify for this exemption, even if one is wholly dependent on the other.

2. If the recipient of the gift or transfer is not domiciled in the UK, the exemption is limited to £55,000.

Annual exemption
Everybody is allowed to give away £3,000 each tax year free of Inheritance Tax. Further, if you do not use up this exemption in one tax year, it can be carried forward and used the next year. However, this carry forward is only valid for one year. It cannot be carried forward any more than one year.

Small gifts exemption
Everybody may give away as many outright gifts as they like in a tax year, up to a total of £250 for each receiver of these gifts. Any gift over £250 is not exempt on the whole amount – not just the excess over £250.

Wedding gifts
You may make wedding gifts free of Inheritance Tax to either the bride or the groom. These gifts are exempt up to certain limits depending on the relationship between the giver and the receiver, as follows:

- A parent   £5,000
- A grandparent or great grandparent £2,500
- Anyone else   £1,000

The bride and groom can also give each other wedding gifts before the wedding up to £2,500 each. After the wedding, of course, all gifts and transfers are exempt, because they are between husband and wife.

Normal expenditure from income
Any regular gifts made from income are exempt, provided that they do not reduce the usual standard of living, and that they are made out of income, not capital.

To qualify for this exemption, it is usually necessary to establish a pattern of gifts over a period of years. It is also necessary to be able to prove that the gifts were made out of income, not capital.

Family maintenance gifts

Gifts made for the maintenance of a spouse, child or dependent relative are exempt. This definition includes illegitimate children, step children and adopted children.

Gifts to political parties and charities

Gifts of any amount to registered charities and the main political parties are exempt from tax – whether made during your lifetime, or passing on your death.

How do you get relief for exempt transfers?
Once again, the key to getting relief for exempt transfers is to keep as full a record as possible. This is particularly important if there is the possibility of establishing a regular pattern of gifts for the 'normal expenditure from income' exception.

PLANNING FOR INHERITANCE TAX

Planning for Inheritance Tax involves decisions which sometimes extend beyond merely financial considerations. These decisions are often very personal by nature, and frequently involve your family – both close family and more distant relatives. It is therefore a good idea to discuss these plans at least with your most immediate family.

Also these decisions, more than any other related to tax saving, are likely to benefit from consultation with professionals – tax advisers or solicitors.

Finally, whatever the government in power, the earlier you make these decisions the better.

Basic considerations

When making any plans to save inheritance tax, you must always ensure that you, or your potential widow or widower, have enough income to live on as comfortably as possible. It is no use living in tax efficient poverty! For this reason planning earlier in your life for an adequate pension is important. It means that there will be less pressure to hold on to assets later in life because they are needed to generate an income.

SHARING ASSETS

Making use of exemptions

As a general rule of thumb husbands and wives should normally share their assets as equally as they can. This is useful not only for Inheritance Tax, but also for other taxes. Each spouse can then make full use of the exemptions and the nil rate band.

Question
Is it always beneficial to divide assets equally between husband and wife?

Answer
This is the general rule. Assets are better shared equally. However, there may be circumstances when one spouse does not want to relinquish a hold on part of the assets. This is particularly noticeable if the marriage itself is not stable.

MAKING A WILL

Apart from the administrative difficulties, not leaving a will can cost your survivors. A will should take into account the Inheritance Tax liability and the way it strikes.

For instance, it could be a missed opportunity if all your estate is left to your spouse. This is because all transfers between husband and wife are exempt anyway. Therefore you could leave an amount up to the limit of the nil rate band (currently £255,000) to the next generation, or other beneficiaries, without any liability.

Again, it must be emphasised that this must only be done if there is adequate money for the surviving spouse to live on. Also, it is not worth passing down more than the nil rate band, because it would mean paying Inheritance Tax earlier than necessary.

It may be possible for the surviving beneficiaries to agree on a 'deed of variation' within two years of the death. This can take effect as if the terms were written in the original will. However, a recent court case has created Inheritance Tax problems for certain variations. It is always best to have a properly drafted will in the first place.

USING LIFE ASSURANCE

This is particularly useful for married couples. The Inheritance Tax charge normally comes on the second death. A life assurance policy written in trust for the survivors can play an important role in providing the funds to pay the Inheritance Tax. If a policy is written in trust, the proceeds on the second death are outside the estate, and therefore do not count towards the estate on which the tax is charged. If it is written on the joint lives, to pay out on the second death, the premium is normally much lower. If a couple start paying the premiums early in their lives the premiums will normally be much lower, and the premiums can become part of their normal expenditure from income and thereby an exempt transfer.

USING TRUSTS

As we have seen, trusts are a technical area which will need the advice and help of a solicitor. Discretionary trusts are the most flexible, since the trustee has absolute discretion to distribute the income and capital. If you give money into a trust you may also be a trustee, so you may retain control over the money given into the trust while it is outside of your estate. However, as we have seen earlier in this chapter, discretionary trusts do suffer tax charges before you die.

There are other types of trust. An accumulation and maintenance trust is normally set up for children or grandchildren. Money given by you into an accumulation and maintenance trust is a potentially exempt transfer. There is therefore no immediate tax charge, and none at all if you survive seven years. Under this type of trust the income must be accumulated for the child until they reach an age between 18 and 25. However, the trustee may distribute income from the trust for the maintenance and education of the children. In order to qualify for the potentially exempt status, the trust must:

- Have beneficiaries who are all grandchildren of a common grandparent, and are aged under 25 at the time the trust is made.

- Ensure that the beneficiaries become entitled to the income of the trust at age 25 at the latest. The capital may pass at a later date.

- Accumulate any income not applied to the maintenance or education of the beneficiaries.

An 'interest in possession' trust is one by which certain beneficiaries may enjoy the income of the trust for their lifetime, and on their death the capital of the trust is paid out according to the wishes of the person who made the trust. If the person who gives the money into this type of trust is also a trustee, he or she may vary the way in which the income of the trust is distributed while he or she is alive.

Whichever type of trust is made, it does have the benefit of being able to protect the assets. If the trust is properly worded it can protect assets from divorce, creditors, or predatory step-relatives. It can even protect the assets from the beneficiary while that beneficiary is young or immature.

MAKING GIFTS

You may take advantage of gifts during your lifetime to reduce the ultimate Inheritance Tax liability on your estate. The combined effect of the nil rate band and the seven year cumulative rule for potentially exempt transfers can often go a long way to mitigating this tax. Gifts do not, of course, have to be made in money, but they can be any other assets. When deciding what assets to give, think about their future potential. The value of the gift for these purposes is the value of the gift at the time it is given. It is therefore more tax efficient to give a gift that is likely to increase in value. This way, any increase in value of that asset comes outside your estate.

If, for example, you have a property that is let to an elderly person, that property would increase in value when the tenant dies. (An empty property is always worth more than a tenanted one.)

There are two points to remember, however.

- First, the gift must be given outright. There must be no 'reservation of benefit'. For instance, if you gave your house to your children, but carried on living in it without paying the full market rent, that would be a gift with reservation of benefit. Any such gifts are not potentially exempt transfers. They are still counted as part of your estate when you die.

- Secondly, you should not give away more than you can afford. It is no use to leave your survivors free of Inheritance Tax if the price is that you live in poverty for the rest of your life. This point has been made already, but it is worth repeating.

MAKING USE OF BUSINESS PROPERTY RELIEF AND AGRICULTURAL PROPERTY RELIEF

There are some very valuable reliefs for businesses and agricultural land. Broadly, these are as follows:

Business Property Relief

Business Property Relief at 100% is given on:

- The business of a sole trader or the interest of a partner in the partnership business.

- Shareholdings in a trading company that is not quoted on a recognised stock exchange.

Business Property Relief at 50% is given on:

- Shares or securities giving control of a trading company that is quoted on a recognised stock exchange.

- Land and buildings, machinery or equipment which
  – you own
  – or a trust of which you are a beneficiary owns
  – but used by either a trading company under your control, or a partnership in which you are a partner.

There are important conditions attached to the business property relief:

1. You must have owned the property at least two years before the gift or death.

2. The company or business must be a trading business. The relief does not apply to investment companies. Nor does it apply to non-business assets. The relief can be restricted if any of the assets have not been used mainly for business purposes.

3. There must be no binding agreement in force for the sale of your interest in the business.

4. If an asset qualifying for this relief is given as a
   potentially exempt transfer, it must still be owned by the
   original recipient and still qualify as a business asset at
   the date of death, if death occurs within seven years.

Agricultural Property Relief

This relief is given on the agricultural value of land and
farm buildings occupied for agriculture. For these purposes
agriculture includes forestry, fish farming, stud farming and
intensive livestock rearing.

Agricultural property relief at 100% is given on:

- Land on which you have farmed for at least the last two
  years, or where you can obtain vacant possession within
  24 months.

- Land farmed by a tenant under a lease that started after
  31 August 1995, and you, the owner, cannot obtain
  vacant possession within one year. You must have owned
  the land for at least seven years, and it must have been
  farmed for all that period.

Agricultural property relief at 50% is given on:

- Land farmed by a tenant under a lease that started
  before 1 September 1995, with the same conditions as
  above.

Conditions also apply to this relief.

1. Not all the assets of the farm qualify as agricultural
   property. The farmhouse is disallowed, and outlying
   'amenity' woodland may also not be allowed.

2. Where agricultural property relief and business property
   relief are both available, the agricultural property relief
   is given first. Most assets in a farming business will

qualify for business property relief, even if they do not qualify for agricultural property relief.

3. If any part of a farm has development value, that land will qualify for agricultural property relief on the agricultural value, and business property relief will most likely apply to the enhanced development value.

4. You are treated as occupying land if you are a partner in a partnership which farms the land, or you control a company which farms the land. Therefore a transfer of shares in a company which you control, and which farms the land, may qualify.

5. If you die within seven years of making a potentially exempt transfer which qualified for agricultural property relief, the land must still be owned by the original recipient and still qualify as agricultural land for the relief to apply.

PLANNING FOR BUSINESS PROPERTY AND AGRICULTURAL PROPERTY RELIEF

The rules, as we have seen, are fairly complex. You should be careful about making sure you comply. For example:

• Make sure that the qualifying periods of ownership apply if you make a transfer or gift of business or agricultural property. In particular, if there has been a transfer between husband and wife, make sure the qualifying period is adhered to after the first transfer.

• The provision about a binding contract for sale is important. If you are in a partnership, therefore, make sure that there is no clause in the partnership agreement which states that, on the death of a partner, 'the surviving partners shall acquire the share of the deceased partner at market value'. It may, however, say that the surviving partners have the option to buy the share of the deceased partner at market value.

- An asset qualifying for business property relief or agricultural property relief is reduced by any loans secured on that asset. Therefore, if there is a mortgage on business property, the value qualifying for 100% or 50% exemption is reduced by the outstanding mortgage. It is obviously better, therefore, if a mortgage could be secured on non business property – say, the domestic residence.

- If a company has been carrying out property development it qualifies for business property relief. However, if properties do not sell, and they are let, that counts as investment income – ie non trading income. The relief could therefore be lost or reduced.

TAX EFFICIENCY AUDIT

1. Do you and your spouse have wills? Are they regularly revised in the light of changing circumstances?

2. Have you passed on as much as you want your children and grandchildren to have before your death?

3. Do you make full use of the exempt transfers?

4. How are your assets divided between you and your spouse? Could they be better divided for Inheritance Tax purposes?

5. Have you considered the use of trusts or life assurance policies?

6. Have you checked with your solicitor that all legal documents (such as partnership agreements, leases etc) comply with the requirements for Inheritance Tax?

11

Stamp Duty

Stamp Duty is a tax which can easily be overlooked when planning a business transaction. Perhaps the reason for this is that it is not a tax on transactions as such. It is, rather, a tax on documents and deeds. Certain documents are by law subject to being stamped, and the duty must be paid. These documents are known as instruments. Stamp Duty is one of the oldest taxes, and the primary legislation is in the Stamp Act, 1891. Stamp Duty is administered and collected by the Inland Revenue.

Perhaps the most common and easily recognised instrument is the document which transfers land or property. This is known as a conveyance. Another common instrument is a stock transfer form, by which ownership of shares in a company is transferred to another person.

When thinking about tax planning in relation to Stamp Duty, remember that:

• If the legal effect of a transaction can be achieved without a deed or document, there is nothing on which Stamp Duty can be imposed.

• If a document does not come within one of the chargeable categories, there is no Stamp Duty payable.

However, many transactions are now paperless – particularly electronic share transfers under the CREST system of the London Stock Exchange. These paperless transactions are subject to Stamp Duty Reserve Tax. Thus

the majority of transactions in quoted shares are subject to
Stamp Duty Reserve Tax (at the rate of ½% of the value of
the transaction). Quoted share dealings outside CREST, and
dealings in shares in unquoted companies, are subject to
Stamp Duty.

Remember – a company buying back its own shares is
making a transaction liable to the Stamp Duty (or Stamp
Duty Reserve Tax) at ½% of the value.

THE BASIS OF THE CHARGE

Stamp Duty is charged on instruments:

* executed in the UK
* or if they are executed outside the UK:
    - they relate to UK property or land, or
    - they require anything done under those instruments
      within the UK, or
    - they are brought into the UK.

The categories of instruments charged are called 'heads of
charge' in the 1891 act. They are:

1. Conveyances or transfers on sale.

2. Leases.

3. Other instruments.

In theory it is possible for an instrument to fall under
more than one of these categories. The Inland Revenue can
choose which category they use to tax it, but it can only be
charged to Stamp Duty once. This would be the 'leading
and principal object' of the instrument.

Warning

It is not possible to write two instruments into one document, and thereby incur only one charge to Stamp Duty. The Inland Revenue are wise to this, and they will charge each instrument separately.

On the other hand, it is sometimes necessary to execute more than one document to give effect to what is in essence a single transaction. In this case, only one of these documents is considered to be a stampable instrument.

CONVEYANCES

A conveyance is the legal document required to transfer the title in land or property from one person to another. Conveyances form the greatest number of instruments chargeable to Stamp Duty. Stock transfer forms are a form of conveyance.

Rate of Stamp Duty on conveyances

Although Stamp Duty is not a tax on transactions, the rate of Stamp Duty on conveyances is based on the value of the transaction – this is known as an *ad valorem* duty. The rates are:

	Rate of Duty
Share transactions	½%
Transfers of other property:	
Value of transaction	
up to £60,000	Nil
from £60,001 to £250,000	1%
from £251,001 to £500,000	3%
more than £500,000	4%

Certain properties in 'disadvantaged areas' have a nil band up to £150,000.

What is 'property'?

Property can be 'real property', such as freehold land or personal property. It can be tangible property (including real and personal property) or intangible property (such as goodwill or patent rights).

Intellectual property transactions (such as trade marks, copyright, design rights, etc) are no longer subject to Stamp Duty. However, when a transaction consists partly of intellectual property and partly of other property, an apportionment must be made on a just and reasonable basis. The Stamp Duty is then only charged on the other property included in the transaction.

What is a conveyance?

As we have seen, Stamp Duty is only chargeable on documents, not on transactions, and then only when the document is necessary to effect the legal transfer of title. So a contract for sale of goods is not stampable, because it is not needed for the legal title in the goods to pass. The legal title in the goods passes on delivery. In the case of the transfer of land and property a conveyance is necessary for the title to pass, so the document is stampable.

It is also necessary to look behind the actual instrument to the commercial reality of the transaction. In a famous case in 1939, the Eastern National Omnibus Company Ltd made a contract not to carry on their business in a particular, defined geographical area. With certain other provisions in the contract, this was held by the judge to be a contract for the sale and transfer of the goodwill. As such, it was legally necessary for the transfer of the title, and therefore subject to Stamp Duty.

What is the value of the transaction?

The value of the transaction for the purposes of Stamp Duty is the normal market value. An instrument must contain a 'certificate of value', failing which it will be subject to Stamp Duty at the highest rate – 4%.

The certificate of value is a declaration to the effect that the transaction is not part of a larger transaction or series of transactions whose aggregate value is more than:

- £60,000 – (or £150,000 for certain properties in disadvantaged areas) in which case it qualifies for the nil rate, or
- £250,000 – in which case it qualifies for the 1% rate, or
- £500,000 – in which case it qualifies for the 3% rate.

Since 1993 it has not been possible to reduce Stamp Duty by exchanging freehold property. If, for example, a house valued at £100,000 was exchanged for a house valued at £50,000 and £50,000 cash, before 1993 the Stamp Duty would have only been chargeable on the £50,000. If the two houses were of the same value there would have been no value at all.

But now Stamp Duty is chargeable on the full market value of each property. However, if the transaction is for the sale of land (such as a builder selling a new house), and the consideration is partly satisfied in kind (eg by the buyer settling part of his liability in kind – ie his old house), then the *ad valorem* duty is only charged on the land being sold. The transfer of the property forming part of the consideration is only liable to the fixed Stamp Duty of £5.

It is possible for an instrument to specify a variable consideration, with a maximum figure. In this case the Stamp Duty is calculated on the maximum payable. It is also possible for the consideration to include a debt taken over by the transferee. The full amount, including any debt taken over, is liable to Stamp Duty.

If the consideration is payable by instalments, Stamp Duty is calculated on the whole amount payable, if it can be calculated. Otherwise:

- If the instalments continue beyond 20 years, Stamp Duty is payable on the total instalments payable within 20 years.

- If the instalments are for a lifetime, Stamp Duty is payable on the payments for the first 12 years.

Warning
The value for Stamp Duty purposes includes any applicable VAT – *even if the VAT is recoverable by the purchaser.*

Tip
It is sometimes possible to apportion the value of property between the value of the land and the value of any 'goods' at the property (eg carpets, fittings, etc). This is particularly useful where the value of the property is just above one of the thresholds. The rate of Stamp Duty is applicable to the whole of the value of the stampable transaction, so to reduce the value of a transaction from £501,000 to £499,000 would reduce the Stamp Duty payable from £20,040 (4% of £501,000) to £14,970 (3% of £499,000). The saving in Stamp Duty has been £5,070, just by allocating £2,000 of the value to goods. However, a couple of points must be borne in mind:

- The value apportioned to the goods must be realistic. You must be able to defend it if challenged.

- When a loan is secured on the property, the lender must be aware of the apportionment. Their security is only against the value of the land. The lender must therefore also give consent to the apportionment.

Planning opportunity
When considering the purchase of a company or its business, remember that there could be as much as 3.5% difference in the Stamp Duty, depending on whether it is the

shares or the assets that are sold. However, buying the shares in a company often incurs a greater risk than buying the assets of that company's business. Each case must be considered on its own merits, but the saving on Stamp Duty could be a major factor when the sums involved are significant.

Relief from Stamp Duty on conveyances between associated companies

If a transaction takes place transferring property between associated companies, there is relief from the Stamp Duty. Companies are associated if:

- one company is the parent of the other
- or both companies have a common parent company.

Since the Finance Act of 2000, a company is the parent of another company for these purposes if it meets all three of the following conditions:

1. It owns beneficially at least 75% of the ordinary share capital of the other company, *and*

2. It is beneficially entitled to at least 75% of the profits available for distribution, *and*

3. It would be beneficially entitled to at least 75% of the assets available for distribution in a winding up.

These are virtually the same conditions which apply to the transfer of Corporation Tax losses within a group of companies.

To qualify for the relief the conveyance must be sent to the Stamp Office for adjudication and approval. Failing this, Stamp Duty is payable in the normal way.

LEASES

The rules for charging Stamp Duty on a lease are as follows.

1. If the lease has a definite term of at least one year, or if it is indeterminate:

   - If all or part of the consideration for the lease (the premium) consists of money or property, the Stamp Duty on that consideration is the same as for conveyances – see above.

   - But, if part of the consideration is for rent, and the rent exceeds £600 a year, there is no nil rate – ie the minimum rate of duty on the premium is 1%.

   - If all or some of the consideration is rent, the Stamp Duty on the rent is determined as follows:
     - If the term of the lease is not more than seven years, or if it is indefinite, then if the rent is £5,000 or less, the rate is nil. If the rent is more than £5,000, the rate is 1%.
     - If the term is between seven years and 35 years, the rate is 2%.
     - If the term is between 35 and 100 years, the rate is 12%.
     - If the term is more than 100 years, the rate is 24%.

2. If the lease has a term of less than one year:

   - If it is a lease of a furnished dwelling house or apartments where the total rent for the term exceeds £5,000, the rate is a fixed rate of £5.

   - In all other cases, the Stamp Duty is the same as for a lease for a year at the same rent.

Agreements for lease

It is often the case that the parties to a lease enter into an agreement to lease some time before they enter into a formal lease. In this case:

- The agreement to lease is subject to the same Stamp Duty as if it were an actual lease.

- When the subsequent lease is made, and it relates to substantially the same property and terms as the original agreement, the Stamp Duty on the lease is reduced by the Stamp Duty charged on the original agreement.

- All leases executed since 5 May 1994 must contain a certificate that there is no prior agreement giving rise to the lease itself.

Surrender of lease

Where a lease is surrendered (whether by a document or by operation of law) Stamp Duty is chargeable as if it were a transfer on sale. If there is no consideration for the surrender, the Stamp Duty is at the fixed rate of £5.

Counterpart lease

A counterpart lease is liable to the fixed Stamp Duty of £5.

Warning
The value for Stamp Duty purposes includes any applicable VAT – either on the premium or on the rent – *and this is true even if the lessee can recover the VAT.*

OTHER DOCUMENTS

Some other documents are chargeable to Stamp Duty. These are:

- a conveyance or transfer other than for sale (eg a transfer by way of gift)

- a declaration of trust, *except*
  – a trust created under a will
  – or a trust under a life assurance policy.

The Stamp Duty on these other documents is at the fixed rate of £5.

Changes to the system

As from 1 December 2003, the system will be changed as follows:

- The existing charge will be replaced by a new charge of 1% on the net present value (NPV) of rental payments under the lease, where the NPV exceeds the zero-rate band of £60,000 (or £150,000 for certain properties in 'disadvantaged areas').

- The zero-rate band threshold for non-residential property will be increased to £150,000, and this will also apply to non-residential leases there the NPV of the rents under the lease does not exceed £150,000.

- Alternative sources of finance used by individuals to buy property will be treated for the purposes of Stamp Duty the same as equivalent conventional mortgages.

- Stamp Duty will be abolished on all transactions involving property other than land, shares, and interests in partnerships.

PAYMENT OF STAMP DUTY

The buyer of the property, or the lessee of a lease, is liable to pay the Stamp Duty. The seller or lessor has no liability or obligation. The Inland Revenue act as the collector of Stamp Duty. The Stamp Office is administered by the Controller of Stamps. All conveyances and transfers on sale must be sent to the Stamp Office whether or not they are liable for Stamp Duty. Documents which must be sent to the Land Registry are sent to the Stamp Office if they are known to need stamping. They are not registered until they are stamped. As it is a duty on documents, the payment is acknowledged by a stamp being impressed on the document, to denote the amount of Stamp Duty paid. The instrument must be stamped within 30 days of being executed.

Adjudication

An apparent anomaly of the Stamp Duty is that the Stamp Office does not necessarily agree that the duty charged is correct, even when it has received the Stamp Duty and stamped a document. To get formal agreement, a document must be adjudicated. This is the process by which the Stamp Office formally assesses the amount of duty.

The adjudication may be:

- compulsory, eg where relief is claimed for a conveyance between associated companies, or

- voluntary – this may be requested by the payer of the duty
    - to ensure that the document has been stamped correctly, or
    - to initiate an appeal (an appeal cannot be made before a formal adjudication has been made).

If the duty on a document has been adjudicated, the document is marked with a special stamp.

Appeals

The payer of the duty may make an appeal once the duty has been adjudicated. The appeal must be made within 21 days of the adjudication, and it must be made to the High Court.

Interest and penalties

See Chapter 12 for details of the interest and penalties due.

TAX EFFICIENCY AUDIT

1. Have you taken Stamp Duty into account when making business plans?

12

Avoiding Penalties, Interest and Surcharges

It would be particularly ironic if, having saved tax through the various means outlined in this book, you were to incur penalties, interest or surcharges. These are extra charges which can be avoided by complying with all the legal requirements, and ensuring that all forms etc are dealt with inside the time limits laid down.

OBSERVING TIME LIMITS

Sending in tax returns

One of the most obvious and important deadlines is that for filing your self-assessment tax return.

Individual tax returns

If you want the Inspector of Taxes to carry out the calculations, you must get the return in by the later of:

- 30 September after the end of the tax year, or
- two months after the tax return has been sent to you.

If you miss this deadline there is no penalty, but you must do your own calculations. The final deadline is the later of:

- 31 January after the end of the tax year, or
- three months after the tax return has been sent to you.

If you miss this last deadline, there is an automatic penalty of £100. The Inspector of Taxes will send you a notice of penalty. If it is more than six months late, the penalty is increased to £200.

If the Commissioners have directed that the tax return must be sent in, the Inspector of Taxes may ask the Commissioners to apply a further penalty of £60 per day after the direction is made. The Inland Revenue have indicated that they will only seek to apply this particular penalty when the tax at risk is believed to be high.

If the tax return is still outstanding a year after the normal last filing date, a further penalty of up to 100% of the tax liability may be imposed.

The total of all these penalties cannot exceed the amount of tax due.

How do you pay penalties?

If you receive a penalty notice, you must pay the amount. A payslip is attached to the notice for you to make your payment. As noted below you may make an appeal, but the Inland Revenue always recommend that you pay the amount due. If the appeal decision goes against you, and you have paid the amount due, there will be no interest added. If the appeal is successful you will be repaid, with interest if applicable.

You may appeal to the Commissioners against these penalties. They may be set aside if you can show that you had a reasonable excuse for the delay. The reasonable excuse must have applied throughout the whole period of failure, not just for part of the period.

How do you appeal against a penalty?

Write to your Inspector of Taxes, to tell them about your intention to appeal. The case will be listed for hearing before the Commissioners, and you will be sent a notice of the date and place of the hearing. You will have to put over your side of the argument, unless you are represented.

Partnership tax returns
If a partnership tax return is sent in late, the same penalties apply as for individual returns. However, there is no restriction as there is for individual tax returns. A fixed penalty is payable whatever the tax payable by the partners, or even if no tax is payable by any of the partners.

Corporation Tax returns
The penalties for late filing of a Corporation Tax return are:

- up to three months late: £100, but this can be increased to £500
- between three and six months late: £200, but this can be increased to £1,000.

In addition to these fixed penalties, there are further tax-geared penalties for further delays:

- between six and 12 months late: 10% of Corporation Tax due
- over 12 months late: 20% of Corporation Tax due.

The circumstances in which the fixed penalties can be increased as stated above are if the company:

- Has been required to make a Corporation Tax return for at least three consecutive accounting periods.

- Has also been liable to Corporation Tax for those accounting periods.

- Has also been liable to a fixed penalty for each of the first two of those accounting periods.

- And is liable for a fixed penalty for the third such accounting period.

In the same way that you may appeal against a penalty on an individual tax return, so you may also make an appeal against a Corporation Tax penalty. The appeal is made to the Commissioners in the same way.

OTHER PENALTIES

Besides the penalties for not observing time limits, there are various other penalties.

Income Tax and Capital Gains Tax

Record-keeping
Failure to keep proper records, and to retain them for the requisite period, can result in a penalty of up to £3,000 for each such failure. There is a right of appeal against this, and the Inland Revenue have stated that they will only seek to apply the maximum penalty in the most extreme cases.

Failure to produce documents in the course of an enquiry
If the Inland Revenue are conducting an enquiry into your tax return, and they have issued a formal notice for you to produce any documents, failure to comply incurs a penalty of £50, with an additional £30 per day for any further delay. This is the maximum that the Inspector of Taxes can impose, but if the Commissioners impose a penalty for this failure, as part of formal penalty proceedings, the maximum penalty is £150 per day.

Corporation Tax

Corporation Tax penalties are similar to but not exactly the same as Income Tax penalties.

Failure to notify the Inland Revenue of liability to complete a return

If:

- you have not received a notice to complete a Corporation Tax return

- but you are liable to tax

- and you do not notify the Inland Revenue within 12 months of the end of the accounting period, then the company is liable to a maximum penalty of 100% of any tax still not paid as at 12 months after the end of the accounting period.

Failure to keep proper accounting records
The maximum penalty is £3,000.

Failure to produce documents in the course of an enquiry
If the Inland Revenue are conducting an enquiry into the company's tax return, and they have issued a formal notice for you to produce any documents, failure to comply incurs a penalty of £50, with a further £30 per day for any further delay. This is the maximum that the Inspector of Taxes can impose, but if the Commissioners impose a penalty for this failure, as part of formal penalty proceedings, the maximum penalty is £150 per day.

Incorrect claims, returns or accounts
The maximum penalty is 100% of any extra tax found to be due.

PAYING TAX ON TIME

Knowing the deadlines
Corporation Tax, Income Tax and Capital Gains Tax due under self-assessment have specific deadlines for payment of the tax. The dates are as described in Chapter 2.

Question
What do I do if I believe that the amount of tax demanded is wrong?

Answer
Write to your Inspector of Taxes to say why you disagree, and pay the amount you think should be payable.

Interest

The Inland Revenue send you reminders shortly before each payment of tax is due. If any payment is made late there is an automatic interest charge on the overdue tax. Interest is charged at the 'official rate' published by the Inland Revenue. A list of the official rates of interest, and the dates for which they applied, is available from your local tax office.

You are sent a 'statement of account' whenever there is tax due, and this shows all tax due, plus any interest, penalties or surcharges due. Interest accrues automatically on any overdue amounts on the statement.

In the case of Corporation Tax interest is calculated at the official rate plus 1%.

Surcharges

In addition to interest on overdue Income Tax, Capital Gains Tax and class 4 National Insurance, the following surcharges are added:

- tax paid after 28 days of due date, but not later than six months – 5% of tax due

- tax paid more than six months after due date – 10% of tax due.

Appeals are allowed against these surcharges, but not against the interest. To set aside the surcharge you must show a reasonable excuse for late payment. *Inability to pay is not accepted as a reasonable excuse.*

Surcharges do not apply to payments on account, only to final payments of Income Tax, Capital Gains Tax and class 4 National Insurance. A surcharge cannot be imposed in addition to a tax-geared penalty.

VAT PENALTIES

There are numerous penalties, surcharges and interest charges for VAT mistakes. Here are some of the more common ones.

Default surcharge

VAT returns are due within a month of the last day of the VAT period. If you are late sending in your VAT return, you are liable to a **default surcharge**. This is the greater of:

- £30, and
- 2% of the VAT due for the first default
- 5% of the VAT due for the second default
- 10% of the VAT due for the third default
- 15% of the VAT due for the fourth and subsequent default.

The default surcharge, however, is only payable when the Customs and Excise issue a surcharge liability notice specifying a surcharge period. This period effectively is a year from the first late delivery of a return.

What this all means is that if you send in a late return, you are not charged a surcharge if you send your next returns in on time for a period of a year. But if you are late again within a year, you are liable for the default surcharge.

Misdeclaration penalty

If you make a misdeclaration of VAT in a return you could be liable to a penalty. However, if you discover a mistake and put it right in a subsequent return, no penalty applies. The penalty is 15% of the tax which would have been lost if the inaccuracy had not been discovered.

This sort of mistake is usually found in the course of a VAT inspection by a VAT officer. Therefore, once you have been informed of a VAT inspection, you cannot then declare an error in a past return to avoid the misdeclaration penalty.

Persistent misdeclaration penalty

If you make at least three mistakes in VAT returns of a 'material amount', then the penalty is 15% of the tax which would have been lost if the second and subsequent misdeclarations had not been discovered. The 'material amount' is the lesser of:

- £50,000 and
- 10% of the gross amount of output tax and input tax added together.

Failure to register for VAT

If you should have registered for VAT but have failed to do so, there are penalties. These are the greater of:

- £50 and
- 5% of the tax lost if the failure goes on for nine months or less, or
- 10% of the tax lost if the failure goes on more than nine months but less than 18 months, or
- 15% of the tax lost if the failure goes on for more than 18 months.

Unauthorised issue of tax invoices

If you issue an invoice purporting to show VAT, but you are not registered, the penalty is the greater of:

- £50 and
- 15% of the amount shown as VAT.

Default interest

If you have not made a return, or the Customs and Excise for any other reason issue an assessment on you, default interest is payable at the official rate (which has been 6.25% from 6 February 1996) on the VAT due under the assessment from the last date on which the VAT return could have been made for the period concerned, up to the date the VAT due on the assessment is paid.

Question
Is there any appeal procedure against VAT penalties?

Answer
Yes, you make your appeal to the Customs and Excise office. They list the case for hearing before the VAT tribunal, an independent body. You will be notified of the date and place of the hearing, and you will have to present your case, unless you are represented.

STAMP DUTY INTEREST AND PENALTIES

If a document that should have been stamped is not, it becomes legally ineffective. It cannot be admitted in a court of law (except in criminal proceedings). If a document is not stamped within 30 days of its execution, the buyer or lessee becomes liable to interest and penalties. Subject to payment of these, the document can then be stamped after the due date, and become legally effective.

For all instruments executed from 1 October 1999, the provisions are as follows:

- **Interest**. Interest is payable at the officially published rate calculated daily from 30 days after the date of execution. Interest is rounded down to the nearest £5, and is not actually charged if it is less than £25. The interest is payable gross, and is not deductible for tax purposes.

- **Penalties**. The maximum penalties are:
  - If the document is presented within one year from the end of the 30-day period, the lesser of £300 or the unpaid duty.
  - If the document is presented more than one year after the end of the 30-day period, the greater of £300 or the unpaid duty.
  - The penalty can be mitigated by the Inland Revenue.
  - No penalty is payable if there is a reasonable excuse for the delay.
  - Penalties are due and payable 30 days after the issue of the determination.
  - The penalties can be appealed against within 30 days.

TAX EFFICIENCY AUDIT

1. Have you given enough attention to your administration to enable you to get all returns sent in on time?

2. Have you arranged your finances so that you can pay all taxes when they become due?

13

Avoiding the Pitfalls

Understandably, the Inland Revenue and the Customs and Excise do not take kindly to cheating. There are regulations covering the two main areas where they stop unfair manipulation of the system. These two areas are **artificial schemes** and **connected persons.**

Artificial schemes are targeted with a range of anti-avoidance provisions. Connected persons legislation governs transactions between connected persons and how they are treated for tax purposes.

ANTI-AVOIDANCE PROVISIONS

On the whole, these provisions arise in response to schemes that are dreamed up by people trying to find loopholes or ways around the law.

There are various cases which have been decided over the years on the way in which certain transactions are taxed. The judgements given in these cases often contain general guidance which is treated by the Inland Revenue as guidelines within which they are able to work.

One of the earliest and most important cases was the Duke of Westminster v CIR. In this the judge's summing up included the statement that 'every man is entitled if he can to order his affairs so that the tax attaching is less than it would otherwise be'. However, a later case (W T Ramsay Ltd v CIR) concerned a complicated series of transactions. At the end of these transactions, all parties to the transactions were in the same position as at the beginning, and the transactions were therefore said to be 'circular'. However, in the course of the transactions a large capital loss had been created. The principle which the judge laid down there was that, where a preconceived series of transactions is entered into to avoid tax, and with the clear intention to proceed through all stages of the transactions at the outset, then the transactions should not be considered in isolation. The commercial reality at the end of the transactions should override the individual transactions taken in isolation.

The later case of Furniss *v* Dawson extended the Ramsay case. This laid down that the series of transactions need not be 'circular' devices, but any particular transaction within a series of pre-ordained transactions could be ignored if the sole reason for it was for tax avoidance, without any other commercial motive.

What all this means is that if someone offers you a part in a complicated deal purely to save tax, it could be challenged in the courts.

Specific anti-avoidance legislation

There are specific provisions of various Tax Acts to counteract different types of artificial transactions. These deal with the following areas (amongst others) for income tax purposes:

- Transactions in securities (eg stocks, shares, etc). These cover such things as:
  - abnormal dividends or distributions from companies to shareholders
  - sales of securities with arrangements to repurchase
  - sales of the right to dividends
  - direct sales and repurchases
  - securities held for one month or less
  - 'manufactured' dividends.

- Transfers of assets abroad, and the right to receive income on those assets.

- Trading transactions at other than market price, if a non-resident is involved or the person holds the item traded as a fixed asset.

- Capital sums in lieu of earnings.

- Transactions in land – whether the profit is liable to Income Tax or Capital Gains Tax.

- Land sold and leased back. Where this happens, the allowance against profits for rent is limited to the commercial market value of the rent. Also, a proportion of the capital sum received for the sale could be taxed.

- Sale and leaseback of assets other than land. The capital sum received could be taxable.

- Loss relief on dealing in commodity futures is not given where there is a partnership which includes a company as a partner, and the main benefit expected from the partnership is setting off loss relief from trading against other income.

In addition, there are anti avoidance provisions for Capital Gains Tax purposes, covering such things as:

- value shifting, including company reorganisations
- company reconstructions and amalgamations
- groups of companies.

The above does not give an exhaustive treatment of the anti-avoidance rules, but it does give some idea of the types of schemes that have been thought up, and the laws necessary to combat these schemes.

CONNECTED PERSONS

The Inland Revenue takes the view that transactions between connected persons are not 'at arm's length'. The general principle is that any transactions between connected persons should be treated as if they were made at a normal market value. If you are involved in a 'connected person' transaction, the onus is on you to justify what the normal market value would be for the transaction carried-out.

So who are 'connected persons'? An individual is connected with:

- a spouse
- a brother or brother-in-law
- a sister or sister-in-law
- a parent or parent-in-law
- a grandparent or grandparent-in-law
- a child or child-in-law
- a grandchild or grandchild-in-law.

A trustee is connected with:

- the settlor of the trust
- any person connected with the settlor
- any company connected with the settlement.

If you are a partner in a business, you are connected with your partners and their spouses and relatives (brothers, sisters, ancestors or lineal descendants).

A company is connected with another company if:

- the same person controls both companies, or

- one company is controlled by a person who has control of the other company in conjunction with persons connected with him or her, or

- one person controls one company and a person connected with him or her controls the other company, or

- the same group of persons controls both companies, or

- the companies are controlled by separate groups which can be regarded as the same by interchanging connected persons.

A company is connected with a person who has control of it. Persons acting together to secure or exercise control of a company are treated in relation to that company as connected to each other.

Question
If I am about to do a transaction with a connected person, what steps should I take to make sure it does not fall foul of the taxman?

Answer
If the price of the transaction is different to the open market value, you should make sure of what the true open market value is. You would then be taxed on the transaction as if that open market value were applied.

How do you inform the taxman?
In order to ensure complete transparency of your dealings with the Inland Revenue, you should write in the space for 'additional information' (box 23.5) on page 9 of your self-assessment tax return (see Figure 8) the details of any connected person transactions.

TAX EFFICIENCY AUDIT

1. Are you considering any 'schemes' to avoid tax liability? If so, have they been cleared by the Inland Revenue, or tested in the courts?

2. Do you know how to obtain open market valuations if you are doing any transactions with connected persons?

14

Planning for Retirement

PROVIDING FOR YOUR RETIREMENT

You may only just have started working for yourself. So when do you start to think about retirement? The answer is – now!

It is never too early to start providing for your retirement. Any delay severely reduces the final benefit when you retire. As a self-employed person you pay class 2 and class 4 National Insurance contributions. Class 2 contributions only qualify you for the basic state pension, and class 4 contributions do not get you any pension at all. They are simply an extra tax on the self-employed. Anyone who has tried to live on the basic state pension will tell you that it is not easy. So how can you start to provide for your retirement?

You can pay pension premiums into a personal pension scheme or into stakeholder pensions. Up to 1988 you could have paid into retirement annuity schemes. These ceased for new contributions in 1988, but if you had a scheme in force then, you can carry on contributing to it. If you are a director or employee of a limited company, you may be able to contribute to a company pension plan. And all these schemes attract tax relief at your highest marginal rate of tax.

Personal pension schemes

The contributions to a personal pension scheme attract tax relief at your top marginal rate of tax. Because of the generous tax relief, there are certain restrictions.

Restrictions

The main function of a personal pension scheme must be to provide a retirement income, therefore you are precluded from taking benefits before the age of 50. There are, however, younger age limits agreed by the Inland Revenue for certain occupations. These include such people as downhill skiers, athletes or sportsmen, dancers, trapeze artists, divers, etc. You must take the benefits by age 75 at the latest.

The provision of life assurance is permitted as a secondary purpose of a personal pension scheme, but it must be subsidiary to the main purpose.

You may also take a percentage of the benefits in the form of a tax free lump sum when you retire and start taking benefits. This is limited to 25% of the fund in your personal pension scheme. The rest of the fund must be used to provide an annuity for the rest of your life (or the joint lives of you and your partner).

Limits of tax relief

You may contribute up to £3,600 per year irrespective of your income, and get tax relief. Tax relief at the basic rate (22% at the time of writing) is deducted at source, whether or not you are a taxpayer. If you pay tax at the higher rate you must claim the additional relief on your self-assessment tax return.

If you pay premiums above £3,600 in a tax year, tax relief on the premiums is only given against relevant income. This includes self-employed earnings, employed earnings and profits from furnished holiday lettings. If you do not have those types of income, you may not pay more than £3,600 per year into a personal pension scheme or stakeholder pension.

There is a limit on the contributions that qualify for tax relief. The limits depend on your age at the beginning of the tax year, and the amount of your net relevant earnings, as follows.

223

Age at beginning of tax year	Percentage of net relevant earnings
up to 35	17.5%
36 to 45	20%
46 to 50	25%
51 to 55	30%
56 to 60	35%
61 to 74	40%

There is also an overall limit to the net relevant earnings figure on which the percentages are based. For the 2003/2004 tax year the limit is £99,000 of net relevant earnings.

Carry back of premiums
You may elect that premiums you pay in one tax year be 'carried back' to the previous year, and the premiums treated as if they were paid in that earlier year. This could be useful if:

- you could not afford to pay the premiums in one tax year, or

- you paid tax at a higher rate in the previous tax year, or

- rates of tax generally were higher in the previous year.

In order to claim to carry a premium back, the premium must be paid before 31 January following the end of the tax year, and you must specify at the time you pay the premium that you wish it to be related back.

How do you carry a premium back to the previous year?
Enter the amount you want to carry back in box 14.3 (for retirement annuities) or box 14.7 (for personal pensions) on page 5 of your tax return (see Figure 4).

Choosing a policy

If you are looking for a personal pension scheme, there are a bewildering number of choices available, and a large number of salesmen, advertisements and websites trying to sell them to you. A salesman employed by the company will be earning his living by the commission he gets from selling to you. Equally, an independent advisor will earn commission.

However, the fact that they earn commission from selling to you does not necessarily mean that you should not invest in it. You can still get good value from a pension scheme. Ask the following questions when choosing a scheme.

What is the basis of the fund growth?
Funds are usually unit linked or with profits. Unit linked means that the premiums you pay buy a certain number of units in a fund or funds provided by the company. Like unit trusts there are different types of funds – typical funds are managed, equity, property, geographical. The prices are quoted in the financial press, and the value of your pension fund at any time is the value of the units multiplied by the number of units you have. This means that the value of your fund can fluctuate.

With profits funds means that the investment profits each year are credited to your account with the company, and you share in the profits of the company as a whole. The profits are added each year by way of annual bonuses. Once given, these bonuses cannot be taken away. The idea is to smooth out the ups and downs of the investment market, so there will not be the sort of fluctuations you get in unit linked policies. Then, when the policy matures, there is also a terminal bonus which is added to the value of the fund.

Windfall payouts
Taking a with profits policy makes you a member of the company. If the company is a mutual company it could give

you a windfall payout if the company were taken over or if it demutualised.

What is the charging structure?
Many companies pay commission and, particularly in the case of regular premium policies, there is a large deduction from your fund in the first year or two. It could then take a few years for your fund to recuperate this deduction. This is known as 'front end loading'. In turn, this of course means that you will lose out if you cancel or suspend the policy in the early years.

How flexible is the policy?
Do you want to pay regular premiums, or a single premium? Does your policy give you the opportunity to suspend premiums if necessary? If you are paying regular monthly or yearly premiums, can you add on single premiums at a later date?

What is the death benefit if you die before taking the benefits?
Some policies would refund you the premiums, with or without interest, if you should die before taking the benefits. However, it is usually much better to have a policy which would pay out the value of the fund.

Taking the benefits
When the time comes to take the retirement benefits from your personal pension scheme, you have several options. The basic set-up is that your contributions over the years have created a fund. You then use that fund to provide an annuity for the rest of your life. You must be careful about choosing the annuity you take. Once you have started it, you cannot change it.

Open market option
You do not have to take the annuity from the same

company to which you have been contributing. You have
the right to take the fund and use it to provide an annuity
from any other company. It is therefore worthwhile looking
at the annuity rates on offer before you take your benefits.
Your company may, however, quote you one figure for the
fund if you take their own annuity benefits, and a lower
figure if you want to transfer the fund to another provider.

Tax free lump sum
As we have seen, you can take up to 25% of the fund as a
tax free lump sum. The figures are slightly different for
retirement annuity policies. It is usually better to take the
lump sum. You can invest it to get an income, and you then
have the capital to use or to pass on to your dependents.
The annuity is an income for the rest of your life (or the
joint lives of you and your partner), and when you die the
fund is lost.

You must use at least 75% of the fund to provide this
annuity, but it is better to have at least 25% of the fund as
capital that you can use.

Increasing annuity
The annuity rate quoted for your fund will be a 'flat rate'
figure. That is to say, once it is fixed the amount of the
annuity stays the same for the rest of your life.

You can, however, decide on an increasing annuity. This
means that the amount of the annuity will increase each
year. This increase can be a fixed amount (say, 3%) or tied
to the official rate of inflation. Obviously, if you choose an
increasing annuity, the starting point will be much lower.
The choice can be something of a lottery. If you live longer,
then an increasing annuity 'wins'. But if you die soon after
taking the annuity, the fixed amount 'wins'.

With profits annuity
A recent refinement of the increasing annuity is the 'with

profit' annuity. The fund continues to grow by investment
gains, and the amount of the annuity increases every year in
line with the profits. The performance of the with profit
fund in which your annuity is invested will determine the
amount by which your annuity grows – so it is likely that
the growth will not be steady.

Unit linked annuity
This is slightly more risky than the with profits annuity.
Your fund is invested in a unit linked fund. The annual
annuity is therefore liable to fluctuations, and can actually
decrease as well as increase.

Guaranteed
You can get the annuity guaranteed for a minimum period,
usually five years. This guarantee means that if you should
die before the end of the guarantee period, the annuity
would be paid out for the rest of the guarantee period to
your dependants.

Sole life or joint lives
You can elect to have the annuity paid out for the rest of
your life, or for the joint lives of you and your partner.
Again, this will obviously affect the amount of the starting
figure. The amount of the annuity can also be varied – it
could, for example, be the full amount of the annuity paid
for the rest of your life, with a fraction (say one-half or two
thirds) paid to your surviving partner.
    A joint annuity can also be for a fixed amount or an
increasing amount.

Phased withdrawal
If you have a series of policies, or if the amount in the fund
is large enough, you can achieve a phased withdrawal. This
means that you can start taking some of the retirement
benefits, and gradually phase in taking the rest, until you

are drawing all the benefits. If you have a series of, say ten policies, you could take out the benefits of one each year for ten years, to gradually build up to a full pension.

This is particularly useful if you want to phase in your retirement by gradually reducing your involvement in the business. If you want to do this the best way is to set up your personal pension scheme as a series of policies right from the start.

Income drawdown

This is another recent innovation. It was introduced when annuity rates were low and taking annuity benefits meant that you were 'locked in' to those rates for the rest of your life. The drawdown facility means that you do not have to take the annuity, but you can draw down a certain amount of the fund and use it as you wish.

By this means you postpone taking the benefits, and you can take them at a time when annuity rates are better. However, you must currently take the benefits by the age of 75 at the latest. This is an area of legislation which is receiving attention, following pressure from the pensions industry.

Stakeholder pensions

This is a form of pension provision introduced in April 2001. It is aimed broadly at people earning between £8,000 and £20,000 per year. However, these pensions are available to anybody. If you are employed, self-employed, or even unemployed, you can still benefit from the tax relief.

You can pay an annual premium of up to £3,600 into a stakeholder pension. The basic rate tax relief is deducted at source, and if you are liable to tax at the higher rate you must claim the additional tax relief on your self-assessment tax return.

SELLING YOUR BUSINESS

You may have mixed feelings about selling the business and retiring. Indeed some people find that they cannot face retiring, and so just go on until they die 'in harness'.

But most people want to enjoy a rewarding retirement. Once you have built up your business you have a valuable asset, which you can sell. It is often true that the goodwill of the business rests with you personally. You have built it up over a number of years. The contacts with your suppliers, competitors, and most of all your customers, make goodwill very personal.

Despite all that, customers realise that you have to retire and most will go with your business successor.

Planning ahead

It is always good to plan as far ahead as you can. Make plans for your retirement at least ten years ahead. Decide whether you want to phase out your retirement, or make a clean break.

Very often you may have a good idea of who you would like to take on the business when you retire. It may well be a member of your family – perhaps the next generation. It may be someone who has worked for you – you may even have trained the person to do the job.

Planning in advance gives you and your successor the chance to smooth out the problems that might otherwise arise. Working with the person who is taking over means that you are able to show them all the aspects of the job – the administration and book keeping as well as the technical side. You are also able to make sure they build up a good relationship with customers and suppliers.

Handling the negotiations

Even if you have known and worked with your successor for a long time, you must handle the negotiations for sale in a business-like manner. Get a solicitor to draw up the agreement for sale, and suggest to the other party that they get an independent solicitor to act for them.

You will have to negotiate a price for the business, how that is to be paid, what is included in the sale and what is not, and the terms of the hand-over. It is quite usual to have a clause restricting the seller of the business from setting up in competition within a certain time period and within a certain geographical area around the business (for example a five-mile radius).

You will also have to be prepared to supply information, such as the business accounts for the last five years.

Advertising the business

It may be that you do not have a buyer ready to take over your business. If so, you will have to advertise it for sale. Some estate agents deal with business sales as well as property sales. There are also specialist business transfer agents who deal only in business sales. They will, of course, take a commission, but they can often get a better price and have access to a larger base of people looking to buy a business. They will have specialist knowledge of the issues involved in selling a business.

PASSING THE BUSINESS ON TO YOUR FAMILY

You might want to pass on the business to the next generation of your family. The best advice is to start preparing for this as soon as possible. First of all, make sure that the next generation actually wants to take on the business. There have been many family arguments caused by a parent's unwarranted assumption that a child will want to take over the business.

If the child does want to do this, they should do all the training they can, and you should support them in it. It may mean some kind of vocational training, or university course.

This could take them out of the business for several years. Be prepared for that.

Creating a partnership

One way of preparing the ground is to bring your child into partnership with you at a point when you feel they are ready for it. Their share of the profit can be determined, giving them an incentive to work for the benefit of the partnership business which will one day be theirs. That way they learn the responsibilities of self employment, and you can eventually pull out without too much disruption. It also makes a phased retirement easier. You can gradually reduce your involvement in the business, while also reducing your share of the profit.

There still remains the financial settlement, and you will no doubt have some capital in the business that your successor must make provision for paying out to you. It is still a good idea to have a solicitor to look at any agreements made, including drawing up the actual partnership agreement.

TAX EFFICIENCY AUDIT

1. Can you afford to delay starting to provide for your retirement?

2. Will you need expert help in choosing a pension scheme?

3. Will you need expert help in deciding how to take the benefits?

4. Who do you want to take over the business when you retire?

5. When do you want to retire?

Glossary

Accumulation and maintenance trust. Special type of trust normally set up for children or grandchildren.

Additional personal allowance. Allowance given to a person not married or not living with their spouse, who is bringing up a child.

Age allowance. The higher allowance given to people over 65.

Agricultural property relief. A relief against Inheritance Tax for agricultural land.

Allowances. Amounts given as a right as deductions from your tax liability.

Anti-avoidance provisions. Tax laws to prevent unfair advantage being taken of 'loopholes' by taxpayers.

Blind person's allowance. Allowance given to a person registered as blind.

Business property relief. A relief against Inheritance Tax for business assets.

Capital allowances. Allowances given for the use of assets in a business or employment.

Capital Gains Tax. A tax on profits made on disposing of assets.

Car benefit. A charge to tax on the value of a car used privately.

Connected persons. People or companies connected to each other so that transactions between them are not 'at arm's length'.

Corporation Tax. The tax charged on companies.

Customs and Excise. The body which administers the assessment and collection of customs duty, excise duties and VAT.

Default surcharge. VAT penalty imposed for late submission of returns.

Discretionary trust. A trust giving the trustee discretion to make payments.

Dividend. An amount paid to shareholders of companies as reward.

Domicile. Permanent status of a person's long term residence.

Enterprise Incentive Scheme. A government sponsored incentive to invest in small businesses attracting tax relief.

Enterprise Management Incentive Scheme. Special scheme to encourage small companies to grant options to key employees to buy shares in the company.

Extra statutory concessions. Concessions published by the Inland Revenue allowing beneficial tax treatment of various items.

Fuel scale charges. A charge to tax on fuel provided for private use.

Gift Aid. A way of making tax-efficient gifts to charities.

Income Tax. The general tax on incomes for individuals and partnerships.

ISA. Individual Savings Account. Type of tax free savings.

Inheritance Tax. Tax due on the transfer of assets from a person – usually on death.

Inland Revenue. The body which administers tax assessment and collection.

Input tax. VAT tax suffered by a business on purchases.

Limited company. A legally constituted company having its own legal identity.

Lower rate bands. Bands of income taxed at lower rates.

Maintenance or alimony relief. Relief given for maintenance or alimony payments.

Marginal rate of tax. The effective rate of tax on the highest slice of income.

Married couple's allowance. The allowance given to married couples living together over the age of 65.

Misdeclaration penalty. Financial penalty for incorrect declaration of VAT due.

Output tax. VAT on a business's outputs, or sales.

Partnership. A body of persons carrying on business together with a view to profit.

PAYE. Pay As You Earn. A system for collecting tax from employed people. Operated by the employer.

Penalties. Financial fines imposed for non compliance with tax regulations.

Persistent misdeclaration penalty. Financial penalty for repeated incorrect declaration of VAT due.

Personal allowance. The basic allowance given to everybody for

Income Tax.

Personal pension relief. Relief given for premiums paid to an approved pension scheme.

Potentially exempt transfer. Transfer from a person's estate which becomes exempt if the transferor survives seven years.

Residence. Status of a person relating to their place of residence – for tax purposes it can be UK resident or non-UK resident.

Restricted allowances. Allowances which are restricted by reference to income level.

Save As You Earn (SAYE). Tax-exempt type of savings plan.

Self-assessment. The system of assessing and paying tax by an individual or a company.

Share options. The right to buy shares at a predetermined price at some future date.

Stamp Duty. A tax levied on the value of transfer of certain assets.

Surcharges. Financial penalties added to tax due for late payment.

Taper relief. A relief given against Capital Gains Tax. Also applied to the reduction in the value of potentially exempt transfers for inheritance tax purposes if the transferor dies within seven years.

Tax credits. Credits for tax deducted at source from investments.

Value Added Tax. (VAT). A tax on business output.

Venture Capital Trusts. Special type of investment attracting tax relief.

Vocational training payments. Relief given for approved vocational courses.

Index

Council Tax, 17
counterpart lease, 204
CREST, 196
Customs and Excise, 17, 18, 112, 125ff, 213

deemed supply, 134
default interest, 215
default surcharge, 213
deregistration from VAT, 124, 127f, 134
director, 44, 98, 101, 166, 177, 222
director's accommodation, 131
director's National Insurance, 102, 164
disclaiming capital allowances, 61ff
discretionary trust, 183, 189
distribution, 183, 202
dividend, 103f, 218
domicile, 94, 184

employee share schemes, 169ff
employment, 21, 166
enquiries, 40, 44, 165, 210f
enterprise management incentive, 178ff
Enterprise Investment Scheme, 14, 66, 153f
entertaining, 130
exemption, 123, 129, 185
extra-statutory concessions, 78

Financial Services Act, 169
financial year, 116
flat rate scheme, 137
food products, 131
forfeiture of shares, 171
freehold land, 198f
fuel scale charges, 133

general principles, 47

Gift Aid, 66
gifts, 186ff, 191, 204
gifts to charities, 187
gifts to political parties, 187
going concern, 100, 111, 112
golden handcuffs, 169
goodwill, 100, 146
group of companies, 122ff, 149, 171, 219
group relief, 121
guaranteed annuity, 228

hold over relief, 152f
home working, 168

income drawdown, 229
Income Tax, 14, 16, 17, 98f, 112
independent financial adviser, 16
inflation, 48, 227
Inheritance Tax, 14, 16, 17, 65, 183ff
Inland Revenue, 15, 17, 18ff, 57, 78, 96, 105, 157, 170, 196, 205
input tax, 123, 128ff
instrument, 196
insurance bond, 51
intangible property, 199
intellectual property, 199
interest, 37, 39, 42, 46, 65, 90, 165, 207ff, 212
interest in possession trust, 184, 190
ISA, 14, 20, 175

joint life annuity, 228

land, 100, 146, 192, 197, 200, 219
lawyer, 16
lease, 193, 197, 203f

237

less detailed tax invoice, 129
life assurance, 16, 189, 204, 223
lifestyle, 13
lifetime transfers, 183
limited company, 18, 65, 91, 98, 100ff, 169, 220, 222
live animals, 131
loan interest, 65
losses, 31, 44, 87ff, 121, 122, 138, 219
lower rate bands of tax, 70ff, 144

maintenance, 65
marginal rate of tax, 50, 222
market valuation, 199, 219, 220
married couple's allowance, 52
matching shares, 144, 173
Memorandum and Articles of Association, 169
misdeclaration penalty, 214
motor cars, 59ff, 132

National Insurance, 17, 36, 98f, 102, 106, 157, 158, 164, 170, 222
national minimum wage, 165

open market option, 226f
options, 170
ordinary residence, 94
output tax, 123, 131ff
overlap relief, 71ff

parent company, 158, 202
participators, 116
partnership, 18, 31, 42f, 65, 98, 105ff, 220, 232
partnership agreement, 98, 105, 194
partnership shares, 31, 42, 98, 105, 108, 173, 232
PAYE (Pay As You Earn), 17,

18, 20, 45, 103, 157ff
payment of tax, 21, 32ff, 45ff, 205, 211
penalties, 42, 101, 123, 165, 207ff
pension contributions, 21, 64, 104, 222
PEP, 20
performance-related achievement, 173
persistent misdeclaration penalty, 214
personal allowance, 47f, 75, 99
personal pension plan, 222f
phased annuity, 228
post-cessation expenses, 67
potentially exempt transfers, 184f, 194
professionals, 15
property, 31, 65, 101, 198
P11, 158, 161
P11D, 87, 165, 167
P45, 158, 159
P46, 158, 160
P60, 164

quoted shares, 197

random enquiries, 40
rates of tax, 52, 123, 198, 224
readily convertible shares, 170, 171
record keeping, 18f, 184, 210f
registration for VAT, 123f, 214
reliefs, 21, 64ff, 145ff
residence, 94, 120
restriction of allowance, 48f, 53
retirement, 75, 104, 174, 176, 222ff
rollover relief, 121, 145

sale and leaseback, 219
savings-related share option

scheme, 175ff
Save As You Earn (SAYE), 175
schemes, 14, 15
seeds, 133
self-assessment tax return, 18ff, 207
self-employment, 31, 222
selling a business, 113f, 230f
share scheme, 169ff
share valuation, 181
Shares Valuation Division, 181
sharing assets, 188
small gifts, 186
sole trader, 99
solicitor, 16, 100, 152, 187, 230
spouse, 165, 184, 185, 188
stakeholder pensions, 175, 222, 229
Stamp Act 1891, 196
Stamp Duty, 17, 100, 112, 196ff, 215
Stamp Duty Reserve Tax, 196f
statement of account, 31, 32, 212
status, 166
Stock Exchange, 76, 181, 196
stock transfer form, 196, 198
subsidiary, 150, 171, 179
surcharges, 207ff, 212
surrender of lease, 204

tangible property, 199
taper relief, 100, 122, 148ff, 171, 177, 178, 181

tax credits, 53, 80
tax free lump sum, 223, 227
tax invoice, 129, 215
TESSA, 20
time limits, 18f, 40f, 43, 44, 88, 148, 155, 180, 207
timing, 75ff, 143
trading stock, 101
transfer of losses, 121
travelling expenses, 80ff
trust, 16, 31, 152, 173, 184, 189f, 204, 220
turnover, 124

unapproved share schemes, 170
unauthorised issue of tax invoice, 215
unit linked annuity, 225, 228
unquoted shares, 197

Value Added Tax (VAT), 17, 18, 105, 111, 123ff, 201, 204, 213
Venture Capital Trust, 65, 155
voluntary registration for VAT, 125

wedding gifts, 186
will, 188
winding up, 202
with profits annuity, 225, 227

zero-rating, 129, 131